Best Easy Day Hikes
San Francisco's North Bay

Help Us Keep This Guide Up to Date

Every effort has been made by the author and editors to make this guide as accurate and useful as possible. However, many things can change after a guide is published—trails are rerouted, regulations change, facilities come under new management, etc.

We would appreciate hearing from you concerning your experiences with this guide and how you feel it could be improved and kept up to date. While we may not be able to respond to all comments and suggestions, we'll take them to heart and we'll also make certain to share them with the author. Please send your comments and suggestions to the following address:

GPP
Reader Response/Editorial Department
P.O. Box 480
Guilford, CT 06437

Or you may e-mail us at:

editorial@GlobePequot.com

Thanks for your input, and happy trails!

Best Easy Day Hikes Series

Best Easy Day Hikes San Francisco's North Bay

Tracy Salcedo-Chourré

FALCONGUIDES

GUILFORD, CONNECTICUT
HELENA, MONTANA

AN IMPRINT OF GLOBE PEQUOT PRESS

FALCONGUIDES®

Copyright © 2011 by Morris Book Publishing, LLC

FalconGuides is an imprint of Globe Pequot Press.

Falcon, FalconGuides, and Outfit Your Mind are registered trademarks of Morris Book Publishing, LLC.

TOPO! Explorer software and SuperQuad source maps courtesy of National Geographic Maps. For information about TOPO! Explorer, TOPO!, and Nat Geo Maps products, go to www.topo.com or www.natgeomaps .com.

Maps created by Trailhead Graphics Inc. © Morris Book Publishing, LLC

Project editor: David Legere
Layout artist: Kevin Mak

Library of Congress Cataloging-in-Publication Data is available on file.

ISBN 978-0-7627-6092-3

Printed in the United States of America

10 9 8 7 6 5 4 3 2 1

*To the Salcedo
and Chourré families.*

Contents

The Hikes
Marin County

Sonoma County

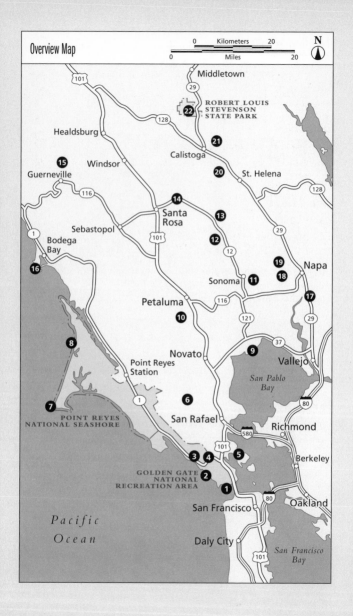

Overview Map

0   Kilometers   20

0   Miles   20

N

Middletown

ROBERT LOUIS
STEVENSON
STATE PARK

Healdsburg

Windsor

Calistoga

St. Helena

Guerneville

Santa
Rosa

Sebastopol

Napa

Bodega
Bay

Sonoma

Petaluma

Novato

San Pablo
Bay

Point Reyes
Station

Vallejo

POINT REYES
NATIONAL SEASHORE

San Rafael

Richmond

Berkeley

GOLDEN GATE
NATIONAL
RECREATION AREA

Pacific
Ocean

San Francisco

Oakland

Daly City

San Francisco
Bay

Napa Valley

Acknowledgments

Thanks to these organizations for their preservation efforts and review of hike descriptions for accuracy: the Golden Gate National Recreation Area; Muir Woods National Monument; Mount Tamalpais State Park; Marin County Open Space District; the Marin Municipal Water District; Point Reyes National Seashore; San Pablo Bay National Wildlife Refuge; the Sonoma Overlook Trail Task Force; Sonoma County Parks and Open Space; Jack London State Historic Park; Sugarloaf Ridge State Park; Sonoma Coast State Park; Armstrong Redwoods State Natural Reserve; City of Napa Parks and Recreation Services; Bothe-Napa Valley State Park; Napa County Regional Park and Open Space District; and Robert Louis Stevenson State Park.

Thanks to the expert editors, layout artists, mapmakers, and proofreaders at FalconGuides and Globe Pequot Press for making this guide the best it can be.

Thanks to these folks for their company and advice on trails: Kerin McTaggart and Juli Lorenc, Ann Peters, Mike Witkowski, Nancy Salcedo, Judy and Jesse Salcedo, and Sitka. Thanks also to Chris Salcedo and Angela Jones; Nick Salcedo; and Sarah, Paul, and Jules Chourré.

Most of all, thanks to my sons, Jesse, Cruz, and Penn, and my husband, Martin.

Introduction

These hikes crisscross my home turf. The trails lead into stories, sound like the laughter of best friends, smell like childhood. It was a delight to document them, and to think about how lucky I am to have grown up with such a beautiful backyard.

That said, selecting the North Bay's "best" easy day hikes presented a huge dilemma—how to choose from all the possibilities? Because I know too much, I've had to edit the best of the best. The trick was to pick hikes that would introduce visitors to the joys of North Bay trails and hopefully turn residents on to new parks or routes. I also felt, for the first time, the conflict of turning strangers on to what are some of my favorite hikes. I have a friend who once told me she'd never forgive me if I wrote about a certain trail. I remain in complete disagreement: Trails are there for everyone to enjoy, and I feel I'm helping both to preserve wildlands and promote a love of the outdoors by writing about them. Then again, I'm hoping that when I venture out, the trail I choose is not overly crowded . . .

In the end, making choices came down to geography, both in terms of terrain and proximity to central locales in Marin County, Sonoma County, and the Napa Valley. The hikes blanket the region, though regrettably some parks and areas had to be excluded. In terms of terrain, some routes are ideal for adventure, some for contemplation, some for a Sunday outing with the family, and others for winding down on a summer evening.

I hope readers will take time to check out the Web sites of the local government and nonprofit organizations that have preserved and/or maintain the trails listed in this guide. On the sites you'll see just how rich the source of wildland exploration is. Don't limit yourself. Explore beyond what's presented in these pages, and make these landscapes the stuff of *your* memories too.

The Nature of the North Bay

Trails in San Francisco's North Bay range from rough and hilly to flat and paved. Hikes in this guide cover the gamut. While by definition a best easy day hike poses little danger to the traveler, knowing a few details about the nature of the region will enhance your explorations.

Weather

Barring major rainstorms, you can hike in the North Bay year-round. The climate is temperate, with few extremes. There are essentially two seasons: the rainy and the dry. The rainy season runs from November to March, and typical daytime highs range from the mid-40s to the mid-60s. Rains are periodically heavy, and on occasion, temperatures in inland valleys fall below freezing and mountaintops are dusted with snow.

The dry season runs from April to October, with temperatures ranging from the 60s to the 80s. In June fog tends to cool the region (the June Gloom). In July, August, and September temperatures jump into the high 70s and 80s, with occasional hot spells.

Only seasonal extremes will preclude use of certain trails. Rains in winter and early spring may saturate routes so that they become muddy and slick, and trails may run through areas subject to closure due to wildfire danger at the end of summer and into fall. Always be prepared for changeable weather—rain, cold, or heat—by wearing layers and packing waterproof gear.

Potential Hazards

While the only critters you're likely to encounter on the trail are butterflies and bunnies, there is the chance you may run across an animal with the potential to cause harm.

Encounters with rattlesnakes and mountain lions are unlikely, but possible. Signs at trailheads warn hikers if these animals might be present. Familiarize yourself with the proper behavior should you run across either a dangerous snake or cat. Snakes generally only strike if they are threatened. Keep your distance and they will keep theirs. If you come across a cat, make yourself as big as possible and do not run. If you don't act or look like prey, you stand a good chance of not being attacked.

Ticks, potential vectors of Lyme disease, also abide in the region. Wear light-colored, long-sleeved shirts and trousers so that you can see the bugs. Remove any ticks that attach as quickly as possible, and seek medical treatment if a rash or other symptoms occur after a tick bite.

A couple of plants that grow in North Bay wildlands may cause problems for hikers. Poison oak (leaves of three, let it be) can cause a nasty, long-lasting skin irritation; stinging nettles prickle and irritate as well. Avoid both by staying on formal trails.

Unpredictable surf and rip currents are common along northern California coastlines. Stay well above the tide line and avoid swimming or wading.

Be Prepared

Hikers should be prepared for any situation, whether they are out for a short stroll through Muir Woods or hiking up the Oat Hill Mine Trail. Some specific advice:

- Know the basics of first aid, including how to treat bleeding; bites and stings; and fractures, strains, or sprains. Carry a first-aid kit on each excursion.

- Know the symptoms of both cold- and heat-related conditions, including hypothermia and heat stroke. The best way to avoid these afflictions is to wear appropriate clothing, drink lots of water, eat enough to keep the internal fires properly stoked, and keep a pace that is within your physical limits.

- Regardless of the weather, your body needs a lot of water while hiking. Drinking a full thirty-two-ounce bottle on each outing is a good idea, no matter how short the hike. More is better.

- Don't drink from rivers, creeks, or lakes without first treating or filtering the water. Untreated water may host a variety of contaminants, including giardia, which can cause serious intestinal unrest.

- Wear sunscreen.

- Carry a backpack in which you can store extra clothing; drinking water and food; and goodies like guidebooks, a camera, and binoculars.

- Many trails have cell phone coverage. Bring your device, but make sure it's turned off or on the vibrate setting.

- Watch children carefully. Waterways move deceptively fast, animals and plants may harbor danger, and rocky terrain and cliffs are potential hazards. Children should carry a plastic whistle; if they become lost, they should stay in one place and blow the whistle to summon help.

Zero Impact

Trails in the North Bay are heavily used year-round. We, as trail users and advocates, must be especially vigilant to make sure our passage leaves no lasting mark. Here are some basic guidelines for preserving trails in the region:

- Pack out all trash, including biodegradable items like apple cores. You might also pack out garbage left by less-considerate hikers.

- Avoid damaging fragile soils and plants by remaining on established routes and not cutting switchbacks. Social trails contribute to erosion problems and create unsightly scars on the landscape.

- Don't approach or feed any wild creatures—they are best able to survive if they remain self-reliant.

- Don't pick wildflowers or gather rocks, antlers, feathers, and other treasures along the trail. Removing these items will only take away from the next hiker's experience.

- Be courteous by not making loud noises while hiking.

- Many of these trails are multiuse, which means you'll share them with other hikers, trail runners, mountain bikers, and equestrians. Familiarize yourself with the proper trail etiquette, yielding the trail when appropriate. If you are hiking with a group, walk single file when passing other hikers.

- Use outhouses at trailheads or along the trail.

Getting Around

All hikes in this guide are within the boundaries of Marin, Sonoma, and Napa Counties. Directions to each trailhead are given from the nearest major city or town, beginning from the nearest major highway.

Major thoroughfares in Marin County include US 101 (north–south), Sir Francis Drake Boulevard (east–west), and CA 1 (north–south).

Major thoroughfares in Sonoma County include US 101 (north–south), CA 12 (east–west), and CA 1 (north–south).

The primary route through the Napa Valley is CA 29/128 (north–south). Silverado Trail also runs north–south.

Public transportation generally doesn't run to these out-of-the-way trailheads. However, if you are interested in getting close to the parks via bus, contact Golden Gate Transit (Marin County) at www.goldengate.org, Sonoma County Transit at www.sctransit.com, or the Napa County Transportation & Planning Agency at www.nctpa.net. Additional public transit information is available at transit.511.org.

Land Management

The following government agencies manage public lands described in this guide and can provide further information on other trails and parks in their service areas.

- National Park Service (www.nps.gov); select a state or park and its site will download. Specific contact information for parks in this guide is provided in the hike entry.

- California State Parks (www.parks.ca.gov); select a park and its site will download. Specific contact information for parks in this guide is provided in the hike entry.

- Marin County Open Space District, Marin County Civic Center, 3501 Civic Center Dr., Room 260, San Rafael, CA 94903; (415) 499-6387; www.marinopen space.org

- Marin Municipal Water District, 220 Nellen Ave., Corte Madera, CA 94925; (415) 945-1455; www .marinwater.org

- County of Sonoma Regional Parks Department, 2300 County Center Dr., Suite 120A, Santa Rosa, CA 95403; (707) 565-2041; www.sonomacounty.org/parks

- City of Napa Parks and Recreation Department, 1100 West St., Napa, CA 94552; (707) 257-9529; www .cityofnapa.org

- Napa County Regional Park and Open Space District, 1195 Third St., Room 210, Napa, CA 94559; napa outdoors.org

How to Use This Guide

This guide is designed to be simple and easy to use. Each hike is described with a map and summary information that delivers the trail's vital statistics including length, difficulty, fees and permits, park hours, canine compatibility, and trail contacts. Directions to the trailhead are provided. Information about what you'll see along each trail, as well as tidbits about the natural and cultural history, is included in the hike descriptions. A detailed route finder (Miles and Directions) sets forth mileages between significant landmarks.

How the Hikes Were Chosen

Hikes range in difficulty from flat excursions to more challenging treks into the coastal mountains. I've selected hikes close to major destinations or population centers, so wherever your starting point, you'll find an easy day hike nearby.

While these trails are among the best, keep in mind that nearby trails may offer options better suited to your needs. Potential alternatives are suggested in the Options section at the end of some hike descriptions.

Selecting a Hike

These are all easy hikes, but easy is a relative term. Some would argue that no hike involving any kind of climbing is easy, but in the North Bay, hills are a fact of life. To aid in selecting a hike that suits particular needs and abilities, trails in this guide are rated easy, moderate, and more challenging. Bear in mind that even the most challenging trail can be made easy by hiking within your limits and taking rests when you need them.

- **Easy** hikes are generally short and flat, taking no longer than an hour to complete.
- **Moderate** hikes involve increased distance and changes in elevation and take one to two hours to complete.
- **More challenging** hikes feature some steep stretches and generally take longer than two hours to complete.

What you think is easy is entirely dependent on your level of fitness and the adequacy of your gear (primarily shoes). Use the trail's length as a gauge of its relative difficulty—even if climbing is involved, it won't be bad if the hike is less than 1 mile long. If you are hiking with a group, select a hike that's appropriate for the least fit and prepared in your party.

Approximate hiking times are based on the assumption that on flat ground, most walkers average 2 miles per hour. Adjust that rate by the steepness of the terrain and your level of fitness (subtract time if you're an aerobic animal and add time if you're hiking with kids). Be sure to add more time if you plan to picnic or take part in other activities like bird watching or photography.

Trail Finder

Best Hikes for History Lovers

Best Hikes for Dogs

Hike Ratings

(Hikes are listed from easiest to most challenging.)

Legend

Transportation

⚬101⚬	U.S. Highway
⚬29⚬	State Highway
————	Improved Road
= = = =	Unpaved Road

Trails

▬ ▬ ▬ ▬	Featured Trail
- - - - -	Trail
————	Paved Trail
→	Direction of Route

Water/Land Features

⬭	Body of Water
⌒	River/Creek
- ˍ - ˍ	Meadow/Marsh
∴∵∴	Sand

Symbols

🅻12	Trailhead
🅻	Ranger Station
■	Building / Point of Interest
🅿	Parking
🚻	Restroom
📷	Scenic View
❓	Visitor Center
🪑	Picnic Area
Λ	Campground
▲	Mountain/Peak
⌣	Bridge
⚑	Gate

Land Management

⬚	State/Local Park
⬚	National Seashore/ Monument

Marin County

1   Headlands Overlook Trails

The Marin Headlands encompass superlative views of the Golden Gate and San Francisco Bay. These two trails, one super easy and the other more remote and challenging, take in those views.

Distance: 0.4-mile loop for Battery Spencer; 1.0 mile out and back for Slacker Hill

Approximate hiking time: 30 minutes for Battery Spencer; 45 minutes for Slacker Hill

Difficulty: Easy for Battery Spencer; more challenging for Slacker Hill

Trail surface: Dirt fire road, broad gravel path

Best seasons: Year-round; be prepared for cold, fog, and wind in any season

Other trail users: Cyclists on the first section of the Slacker Hill Trail

Canine compatibility: Dogs not permitted

Fees and permits: No fees or permits required

Schedule: Open daily, sunrise to sunset

Trailhead facilities: Battery Spencer has a roadside parking area, restrooms, and information signboards. No facilities at Slacker Hill; parking is in pullouts alongside McCullough Road.

Maps: USGS San Francisco North; online at www.nps/gov/goga

Other: A road improvement project on the headlands runs through 2011. Check www.projectheadlands.gov for information on road closures and trail access.

Trail contacts: Golden Gate National Recreation Area (GGNRA), Fort Mason, Building 201, San Francisco, CA 94123-1307; (415) 561-3000; www.nps.gov/goga. Golden Gate National Parks Conservancy; (415) 561-3000; www.parksconservancy.org.

Finding the trailhead: Heading southbound on US 101 from Mill Valley and Sausalito toward San Francisco, take the Sausalito/ GGNRA exit, the last Marin exit before the Golden Gate Bridge. At the stop sign turn left, then quickly right, onto Conzelman Road. The Battery Spencer trailhead is on the left at 0.4 mile. To reach Slacker Hill, climb 1.2 miles to the junction of Conzelman and McCullough Roads and turn right onto McCullough. The trailhead is the gated fire road on the right at 0.1 mile. GPS (Battery Spencer): N37 49.769' / W122 29.024'; GPS (Slacker Hill): N37 50.086' / W122 29.674'

The Hikes

You see them everywhere—those iconic photos of the Golden Gate Bridge with the sparkling San Francisco skyline behind. No need to purchase a postcard if you venture on either of these short trails in the Marin Headlands. You can snap the photo, but the images in your mind's eye will be just as lasting.

The Marin Headlands, part of the Golden Gate National Recreation Area, form a steep, brushy rampart on the north side of the strait at the mouth of San Francisco Bay. The views from its hilltops look south across the water to San Francisco and Lands End, and east into the bay over Alcatraz and Treasure Islands. You can also look west out to sea, where the Farallon Islands pop like sharp teeth from the water, only visible on the clearest days.

The headlands have proved valuable not just for sight-seeing, but also for military defense. A succession of batteries, replaced as they became obsolete, were constructed in these hills (as well as on the San Francisco peninsula and islands in the bay). At Battery Spencer you can tour the remnants of both a turn-of-the-twentieth-century battery, with a broad concrete apron spreading down toward the

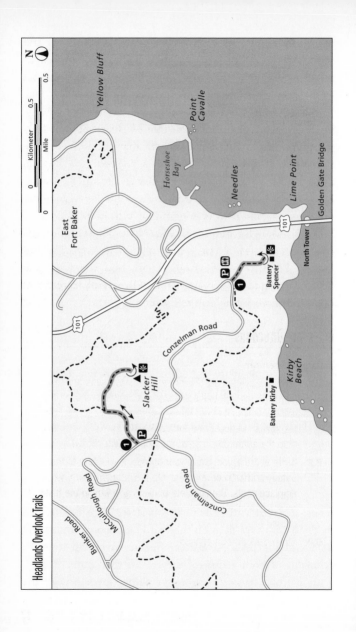

Headlands Overlook Trails

N

Kilometer
0   0.5

Mile
0   0.5

Yellow Bluff

East
Fort Baker

Horseshoe Bay

Point
Cavalle

Needles

Lime Point

101

North Tower

Golden Gate Bridge

Conzelman Road

Battery Spencer

P

Slacker
Hill

P

Kirby
Beach

Battery Kirby

McCullough Road

Bunker Road

Conzelman Road

north tower of the Golden Gate Bridge, and the brick and earthwork Ridge Battery that preceded it, dating back to the Civil War. The short trail looping through the batteries is very popular, so be prepared for company.

Slacker Hill is not for slackers, and not for the average sightseer either. This is a hiker's trail—a steep but mercifully short climb to a windswept summit that you'll likely have all to yourself. You'll also have views, sweeping 360 degrees from the Pacific to San Francisco Bay to Mount Tamalpais. Lush coastal scrub lines the trail, with wildflowers blooming in springtime and raptors migrating overhead in fall.

Options: The headlands offer miles of trail through coastal scrub and military batteries. Visit Hawk Hill at Battery 129 to combine history with bird watching, and venture down to Rodeo Lagoon and Beach for recreational opportunities fronting on the Pacific.

Miles and Directions

Battery Spencer

0.0 Start by walking past the information signboards and rest-rooms. Where the trail splits stay left, up the stairs, on the high route (you'll return through the batteries below). Pass the scenic overlook, and then follow the broad gravel path atop the earthworks toward the Golden Gate Bridge.

0.2 Arrive at the apron. Snap your photos, then return to the battery and drop down stairs into the structure, with gun emplacements. The concrete bunkers give way to the rustic brick fortifications of Civil War–era Ridge Battery as you return.

0.4 Arrive back at the trailhead.

Slacker Hill

0.0 Start by passing the gate and heading up the broad dirt road.

0.2 Pass a sign marking the habitat of the mission blue butterfly at the junction with the Coastal Trail. Go right and uphill on the Slacker Trail.

0.4 Pass a gate blocking a side trail, staying right on the narrowing Slacker route.

0.5 Arrive on the summit (840 feet) and enjoy the views. Retrace your steps to return.

1.0 Arrive back at the trailhead.

2 Tennessee Valley Trail

Follow an easy route through onetime ranchland and a brushy headlands valley to little Tennessee Cove. Bordered by a steep cliff on the south and imposing hillsides on the north, the small beach opens onto the turbulent Pacific.

Distance: 3.4 miles out and back
Approximate hiking time: 2 hours
Difficulty: Easy
Trail surface: Paved road, dirt road, singletrack
Best seasons: Year-round
Other trail users: Trail runners; cyclists and equestrians on the Tennessee Valley Trail (Lower Tennessee Valley Trail is hikers only)
Canine compatibility: Dogs not permitted
Fees and permits: No fees or permits required
Schedule: Open daily, sunrise to sunset
Trailhead facilities: Large parking area; picnic sites, restrooms, information signboard, trashcans. The lot fills quickly on weekends; overflow parking is available alongside the road.
Maps: USGS Point Bonita; map posted at the trailhead; online at www.nps/gov/goga
Other: Currents and surf in Tennessee Cove are turbulent. Swimming and wading are not advised.
Trail contacts: Golden Gate National Recreation Area, Fort Mason, Building 201, San Francisco, CA 94123-1307; (415) 561-4700; www.nps.gov/goga. Golden Gate National Parks Conservancy; (415) 561-3000; www.parksconservancy.org.

Finding the trailhead: From US 101 in Mill Valley, take the CA 1/Stinson Beach exit. Follow CA 1 for 0.5 mile to Tennessee Valley Road. Turn left (southwest) and follow Tennessee Valley Road for 1.7 miles to the parking area and trailhead. GPS: N37 51.628' / W122 32.144'

The Hike

This tiny cove is one of the premier destinations in the Golden Gate National Recreation Area. Its dark sand beach, perhaps 300 yards long, opens on the ocean and backs up to a small lagoon. Sea-sculpted cliffs form an imposing frame for the views.

The beach—like cove, valley, and trail—is named for the shipwrecked steamer *Tennessee*. According to the National Marine Sanctuaries shipwreck database, the *Tennessee* attempted to reach the Golden Gate in heavy fog, only to be dragged off course by strong currents. The captain realized the ship's dire circumstances just in time and beached the vessel in the little cove, saving passengers and cargo. Heavy surf destroyed any chance of making the *Tennessee* seaworthy again, and within two weeks salvage crews and waves had consumed the ship. All that remains is the engine, which can sometimes be spotted off the beach at low tide.

The main trail leading down to the beach is broad and easy, perfect for a family outing. The hikers-only Lower Tennessee Valley Trail, which runs parallel to the broader track, is described here, though you may choose to stick to high ground after a rainstorm. The lower dirt single-track sticks close to the willow-shrouded stream that flows through Tennessee Valley to the sea.

The upper and lower trails merge just before you reach the lagoon, a harbor for a variety of shore- and seabirds. The route leads around the north side of the thickly vegetated shoreline (look for dense clusters of nonnative white calla lilies in spring) then crosses the outlet stream to the lovely little beach. If you'd like a loftier viewpoint, a steep

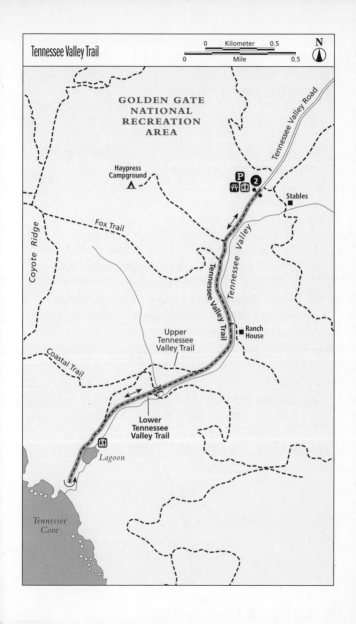

Tennessee Valley Trail

0   Kilometer   0.5

0   Mile   0.5

N

GOLDEN GATE
NATIONAL
RECREATION
AREA

Tennessee Valley Road

Haypress
Campground

P

2

Stables

Fox Trail

Coyote Ridge

Tennessee Valley

Tennessee Valley Trail

Ranch
House

Upper
Tennessee
Valley Trail

Coastal Trail

Lower
Tennessee
Valley Trail

Lagoon

Tennessee
Cove

path leads up to a bench and overlook near an abandoned bunker.

Miles and Directions

0.0 Start down the paved path; a trail sign says that Tennessee Beach is 1.5 miles ahead (it's actually a bit farther).

0.2 Pass a bench at the junction with the Haypress Camp Trail. Stay straight on the paved roadway.

0.3 The Fox Trail breaks to the right; again, stay straight on the paved trail.

0.6 Pass a former ranch house behind a windbreak of eucalyptus. At the trail Y, go right on the signed Tennessee Valley Trail, now a gravel road. The left route leads to a picnic site.

0.9 At the junction of the Lower and Upper Tennessee Valley Trails, stay left on the hikers-only lower trail.

1.1 Cross a bridge to the junction with the Coastal Trail, which leads to Wolf Ridge and Rodeo Beach. Continue straight on the Lower Tennessee Valley Trail.

1.4 Merge with the upper trail, bearing left toward the sea. Pass a call box and picnic site, then hitch up over a rise to the lagoon.

1.7 The trail splits at the west end of the lagoon; stay right to the beach. Enjoy the sights; venture up to the viewpoint, then retrace your steps.

3.4 Arrive back at the trailhead.

3 Muir Woods Loop Walk

Paved paths and scenic bridges lace through a forest of some of the oldest, tallest, and most glorious trees in California. A magnet for tourists and locals alike, Muir Woods National Monument provides the quintessential redwood experience.

Distance: 1.2-mile lollipop (1.6-mile lollipop from overflow parking)

Approximate hiking time: 1 hour (or more)

Difficulty: Easy

Trail surface: Paved

Best seasons: Year-round

Other trail users: None

Canine compatibility: Dogs not permitted

Fees and permits: Entrance fee

Schedule: Open daily, 8:00 a.m. to sunset

Trailhead facilities: Restrooms, visitor center, cafe, gift shop, trashcans, water

Maps: USGS San Rafael; map in brochure available at trailhead; online at www.nps.gov/muwo

Other: The paved path is wheelchair accessible.

Special considerations: Muir Woods is massively popular, so expect traffic congestion, full parking lots, and crowded trails, especially on weekends. To avoid traffic and parking woes, take the Route 66 Muir Woods Shuttle (schedule at goldengate.org/news/transit/muirwoods.php). The shuttle runs from May to September.

Trail contacts: Muir Woods National Monument, Mill Valley, CA 94941; (415) 388-2595; www.nps.gov/muwo. Golden Gate National Parks Conservancy; (415) 561-3000; www.parksconservancy.org.

Finding the trailhead: From US 101 in Mill Valley, take the CA 1/Stinson Beach exit. Follow CA 1 for 0.5 mile to the traffic light at Tam Junction. Turn left (west) to continue on CA 1; go 2.7 miles to the Panoramic Highway. Go right on Panoramic Highway and travel 0.8 mile to Muir Woods Road. Turn left onto Muir Woods Road and go

1.3 miles to the park's entrance. If the main lot is full, continue down the road to overflow parking at the Dipsea trailhead. Additional parking is available along the road. GPS: N37 53.563' / W122 34.366'

The Hike

Muir Woods National Monument does a standout job of living up to the legacy of its namesake, famed naturalist and wilderness advocate John Muir. The monument protects a beautiful pocket of old-growth redwood trees in a steep canyon at the foot of Mount Tamalpais. Spared by inaccessibility, the trees escaped the voracious appetite for lumber that decimated other redwood groves in the Bay Area during and following the gold rush.

Winter rains and dense summertime fog—the typical weather pattern for the northern California coast—create the perfect habitat for coast redwoods. In winter, rainfall replenishes streams around which the redwoods thrive. In summer, fog condenses on needles and drops to the forest floor to water the trees. While the related giant sequoias hold the title of the largest living things on earth, coast redwoods are taller, with the tallest measured at more than 370 feet. Redwoods aren't the only plants thriving in Muir Woods: Several varieties of fern, riparian stalwarts like alder and buckeye, and springtime wildflowers like redwood violet, broad-leafed trillium, and redwood sorrel grow in the understory.

The main paved circuit of the valley floor is described here. On weekends it's a human highway, albeit a quiet, reverent one. You stand a good chance of seeing someone hug a tree—the green spell of the forest invites that. Without doubt you'll see hikers standing open-mouthed with their heads tilted back, staring up through camera lenses into the canopy.

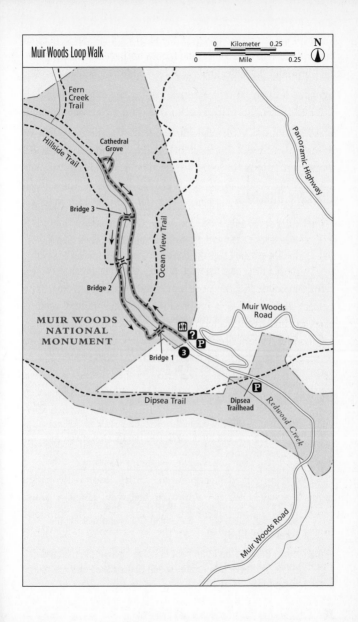

Muir Woods Loop Walk

0   Kilometer   0.25

0   Mile   0.25

N

Fern
Creek
Trail

Hillside Trail

Cathedral
Grove

Bridge 3

Bridge 2

Ocean View Trail

Panoramic Highway

MUIR WOODS
NATIONAL
MONUMENT

Muir Woods
Road

?

P

3

Bridge 1

Dipsea Trail

Dipsea
Trailhead

P

Redwood Creek

Muir Woods Road

The route can be hiked in either direction. It is described here traveling counterclockwise, up the east side of Redwood Creek and down the west side. The trail is lined with benches and interpretive signs. Along the way you'll pass the Pinchot Tree, Cathedral Grove, and Bohemian Grove. Opportunities to venture farther into the monument, or into neighboring state and national park land, exist along the route. Check the trail map, and explore at will.

Miles and Directions

0.0 Start at the entry kiosk. Stay right on the boardwalk, passing the visitor center and more restrooms. (If you've parked in the Dipsea Trail parking lot, follow the paved creekside path for 0.2 mile, past the main parking lot, to the entrance.)

0.1 At Bridge 1, stay right on the boardwalk. Check out the timeline on an enormous redwood slice, dating back to the year AD 1. The paved path begins.

0.2 Pass the Pinchot Tree, named for Gifford Pinchot, conservationist and the first chief of the USDA Forest Service. The Ocean View Trail takes off to the right. Stay straight on the paved path.

0.3 At Bridge 2, stay right on the pavement.

0.5 At Bridge 3, stay right again, entering Cathedral Grove.

0.6 Reach the end of Cathedral Grove. The trail forks; stay left, circling the grove.

0.8 Back at Bridge 3, go right and across the creek, then go left and downstream.

1.0 At the Hillside Trail junction at Bridge 2, stay straight on the pavement, entering the Bohemian Grove and passing the Bicentennial Tree.

1.2 Cross Bridge 1 and turn right to arrive back at the trailhead. (If you've traveled from the Dipsea parking area, retrace your steps to the lot at 1.6 miles.)

4 Mount Tamalpais Summit Tour

Two short trails—the Verna Dunshee Memorial Trail and the Plank Trail—allow hikers to circumnavigate the highest peak in Marin County and then climb to its summit, enjoying panoramic views every step of the way.

Distance: 1.4-mile lollipop (Verna Dunshee Memorial Trail, 0.8-mile loop; Plank Trail, 0.6 mile out and back)

Approximate hiking time: 1 hour

Difficulty: Easy for Verna Dunshee loop; more challenging for Plank Trail due to uneven trail surface and elevation gain

Trail surface: Pavement, wooden planks, rocky singletrack

Best seasons: Year-round; vistas in winter on clear days may reach to the Sierra Nevada

Other trail users: None

Canine compatibility: Leashed dogs permitted

Fees and permits: Parking fee

Schedule: Open daily, 7:00 a.m. to sunset

Trailhead facilities: Huge parking area; restrooms, picnic facilities, water, trashcans, information signboards. A visitor center, recreation stand, gift shop, and gravity car barn are open on weekends. A snack bar is also open weekends during summer.

Maps: USGS San Rafael; online at www.parks.ca.gov

Other: The Verna Dunshee Trail is accessible.

Special considerations: Be prepared for variable weather. The summit of Mount Tam, even in summer, can be downright arctic when the fog moves in. It can also be hot when coastal areas are socked in. Dress in layers.

Trail contacts: Mount Tamalpais State Park, 801 Panoramic Highway, Mill Valley, CA 94941; (415) 388-2070; www.parks.ca .gov

Finding the trailhead: From US 101 in Mill Valley, take the CA 1/Stinson Beach exit. Follow CA 1 for 0.5 mile to the traffic light at Tam Junction and turn left (west) to stay on CA 1. Continue 2.7 miles to the Panoramic Highway. Turn right onto Panoramic Highway and go 5.4 miles to Pantoll Road. Follow Pantoll Road for 1.5 miles to East Ridgecrest Boulevard. Turn right onto East Ridgecrest and go 3.1 miles to the road's end at the trailhead parking lot. GPS: N37 55.800' / W122 34.551'.

The Hike

The slopes of the Sleeping Lady (aka Mount Tamalpais) are boldly dressed in a rich, green recreational cloak. Trails are draped like ribbons across its forested skirts, and on the summit, a pair of paths offer hikers a chance to look down on the entire San Francisco Bay Area.

Mount Tam has long been the center of attention for people living in her shadow. The name is derived from a Coast Miwok term meaning bay or coast mountain, and with ridges sweeping to both the Pacific and into the bay, the moniker rings true. The mountain became a recreational mecca during the gold rush, and it has been a magnet for hikers and sightseers—and most recently mountain bikers—ever since.

The summit trails are part of a park trail system that exceeds 50 miles—and these trails link up with hundreds of miles more in the neighboring Golden Gate National Recreation Area and on Marin Municipal Water District lands. One of the most popular Mount Tam hikes (far too long to be considered easy) follows the route of the Mount Tamalpais Scenic Railway, known as the "Crookedest Railroad in the World" because the tracks doubled back on themselves so often. Gravity cars plunged from the peak down into Muir Woods; one of these cars has been preserved at the summit.

The accessible Verna Dunshee Memorial Trail, dedicated to the memory of a park system heroine, can be traveled in either direction. Circling the peak on a sunny day, the panoramic views will stop you in your tracks time and time again. From the Farallon Islands on the Pacific horizon to the San Francisco skyline, from the slopes of Mount Diablo to those of Mount St. Helena—you'll see it all from this easy, often-crowded paved track.

The Plank Trail leads up to the summit proper, with the planks that form the trailbed giving way to a rock singletrack that might require a bit of scrambling in spots. The stone-walled Gardner Fire Lookout, built in 1937, crowns the mountain, and a rest spot on any side of the squat structure will afford fabulous views.

The Verna Dunshee Memorial Trail can be hiked in either direction; it is described here counterclockwise. The crowds are the biggest challenge you'll face on the trail, with large groups rudely blocking the path on occasion. Be considerate of your fellow hikers by walking single file on the narrow trail.

Miles and Directions

0.0 Start to the right, dropping below a picnic site to the paved path. Views south to the Golden Gate, San Francisco, and Ocean Beach are in your sights.

0.3 As you round the mountain, vistas of San Pablo Bay, bay-side Marin cities, and the Richmond–San Rafael Bridge are served up. Pass beneath a rock overhang. At the Temelpa Trail junction, stay left on the paved Verna Dunshee Memorial Trail.

0.4 Pass stairs and a social path to a viewpoint, staying on the paved track. Benches overlook the rolling hills to the north, with the tiered reservoirs of the Marin Municipal Water District glittering below.

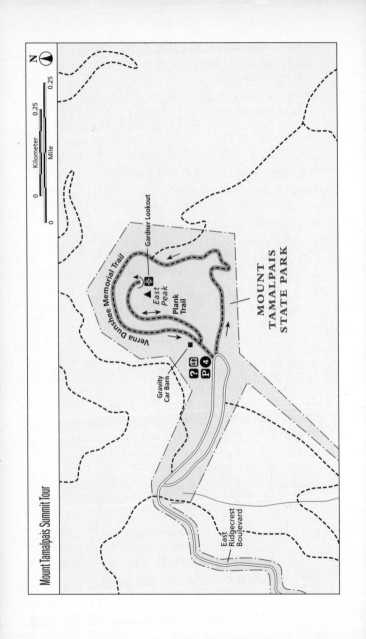

Mount Tamalpais Summit Tour

N

0   0.25
Kilometer

0   0.25
Mile

Gravity Car Barn

Verna Dunshee Memorial Trail

Gardner Lookout

East Peak

Plank Trail

MOUNT TAMALPAIS STATE PARK

East Ridgecrest Boulevard

0.6 Now on the west side, enjoy views of Tam's middle peak, topped with radio towers. Pass a defunct trail, staying right on the paved path.

0.8 Pass the gravity car barn. If the barn is open, check out the interpretive displays. Close the loop, then pick up the signed Plank Trail, which goes left and uphill from the gravity car barn.

0.9 The plank ramp gives way to stairs, then a rocky path. A switchback presents views across the bay.

1.1 Round another switchback and climb stairs to the summit lookout at 2,571 feet. Check out the views, then retrace your steps.

1.3 From the base of the Plank Trail, continue straight toward the parking area.

1.4 Arrive back at the trailhead.

5 Phyllis Ellman and Loop Trails (Ring Mountain Open Space Preserve)

This little preserve straddles the divide between suburban Tiburon and Corte Madera and features a pair of hiking-only trails with spectacular views of San Francisco and San Pablo Bays.

Distance: 2.0-mile loop
Approximate hiking time: 1.5 hours
Difficulty: Moderate due to elevation change
Trail surface: Dirt singletrack
Best seasons: Year-round
Other trail users: Mountain bikers allowed on fire roads only
Canine compatibility: Leashed dogs permitted
Fees and permits: No fees or permits required
Schedule: Open daily, sunrise to sunset

Trailhead facilities: Parking alongside Paradise Drive; information signboard
Maps: USGS San Quentin; online map at www.co.marin.ca.us/depts/PK/Main/pos/parks.cfm
Other: The route crosses several seasonal streams that can be muddy and slick in wet weather.
Trail contacts: County of Marin Parks and Open Space Department, 3501 Civic Center Dr., Room 260, San Rafael, CA 94903; (415) 499-6387; www.co.marin.ca.us/depts/PK/Main/pos/parks.cfm

Finding the trailhead: From US 101 in Corte Madera, take the Paradise Drive exit. Head east on Paradise Drive for 1.5 miles to the trailhead on the right (south) side of the road. GPS: N37 55.264' / W122 29.676'

The Hike

Ring Mountain is a startlingly beautiful dollop of wilderness on a ridge above the Tiburon Peninsula. On a clear day, vistas from the saddle stretch north across the tidal wetlands of the Corte Madera Marsh State Ecological Reserve to San Quentin, and south across San Francisco Bay to the city skyline. Pair the views with the pleasing topography, and Ring Mountain rises well above the realm of ordinary.

Phyllis Ellman, a dynamo of a conservationist who passed away in 2009, was the driving force behind the preservation of Ring Mountain in the 1970s. She and her husband, George, worked tirelessly—well into retirement—on a variety of preservation and conservation issues, many focused in Tiburon and around Glen Ellen, where the couple spent their golden years.

This loop begins on a trail named in Ellman's honor, climbing through a large bowl of grassland through terrain that supports a number of species uniquely adapted to serpentine soils. This greenish stone—California's official state rock—is the catalyst for conditions that permit the Tiburon mariposa lily to thrive. The lily grows here and no place else on Earth.

The route tops out at Turtle Rock. From the summit the Loop Trail drops down through copses of oaks watered by seasonal streams to link up again with the Phyllis Ellman Trail.

A number of social trails intersect both trails, a situation that no doubt would disappoint the park's founding mother. Do your best to remain on the signed official track to preserve the ecology of the grasslands. Interpretive markers line the route, but interpretive guides may not be available at the trailhead.

Options: Marin County's open space department oversees

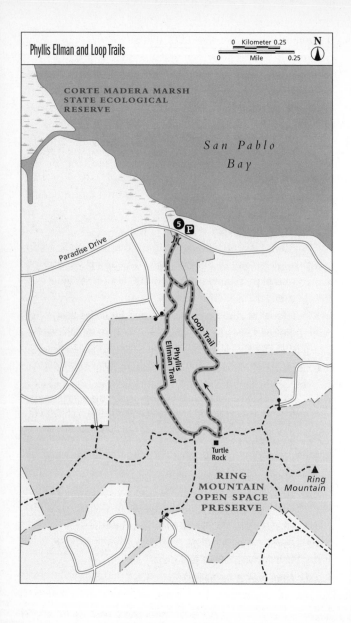

Phyllis Ellman and Loop Trails

0 Kilometer 0.25
0 Mile 0.25

N

CORTE MADERA MARSH
STATE ECOLOGICAL
RESERVE

San Pablo
Bay

5 P

Paradise Drive

Loop Trail

Phyllis
Ellman
Trail

Turtle
Rock

RING
MOUNTAIN
OPEN SPACE
PRESERVE

Ring
Mountain

a number of preserves, including a huge interlocking expanse in the San Geronimo Valley and the popular Bothin Marsh wetland and trail. Visit the Web site and explore.

Miles and Directions

0.0 Start by passing the fence and information signboard, then cross a bridge and climb to the trailhead signs. Head uphill on the singletrack Phyllis Ellman Trail.

0.2 At the junction of the Loop and Phyllis Ellman Trails, stay right on the Ellman track.

0.3 Wood stairs lead up to a fence segment and the junction with a trail into the adjacent neighborhood. A social trail heads straight uphill. Stay left on the Ellman track.

0.5 Trails merge above a set of stairs and interpretive post #15. Go left, past a trail marker, then stay right on the signed Ellman Trail.

0.7 Stay left at trail junctions low in the rock-studded bowl, passing a trail sign and post #14. A steep rocky pitch leads to a trail arrow pointing up and right toward the ridgeline.

1.0 Reach the ridgetop. Cross the saddle to the singletrack leading left and up to Turtle Rock.

1.1 Arrive at Turtle Rock. Cross the fire road on the north side of the rock to the signed Loop Trail. Climb through a cluster of oaks and stay left to drop back into the bowl. Mount Tamalpais comes into view.

1.3 Follow arrows and interpretive posts down to wooden bridges that span a seasonal stream.

1.6 The trail widens as it approaches the stream again. Stone and wood steps lead down alongside the creek past yet another social trail. Stay left and head downhill.

1.8 Reach the junction of the Phyllis Ellman and Loop Trails. Turn right and retrace your steps.

2.0 Arrive back at the trailhead.

6 Lake Lagunitas Loop

A circuit around Lake Lagunitas rambles through redwood groves and serves up nice views of the wooded slopes of Mount Tamalpais—and may include glimpses of great blue herons along the shoreline and turtles on the floats near the dam.

Distance: 1.7-mile loop
Approximate hiking time: 1 hour
Difficulty: Easy
Trail surface: Dirt fire road
Best seasons: Year-round
Other trail users: Trail runners, mountain bikers, equestrians
Canine compatibility: Leashed dogs permitted
Fees and permits: Parking fee
Schedule: Open daily, sunrise to sunset
Trailhead facilities: Parking area; picnic sites, restrooms, water, trashcans, information signboards
Maps: USGS San Rafael; online watershed map at www.marinwater.org/documents/2008.08.29_VstrMap_b_w.pdf
Other: No swimming is permitted. Fishing is catch-and-release only.
Trail contacts: Marin Municipal Water District, 220 Nellen Ave., Corte Madera, CA 94925; (415) 945-1455; www.marinwater.org

Finding the trailhead: From US 101 in Corte Madera, take the Sir Francis Drake Boulevard/San Anselmo exit. Follow Sir Francis Drake for 5.8 miles to Fairfax. Go quickly left, then right, onto Broadway, and drive 0.1 mile to the junction with Bolinas Road. Turn left and follow Bolinas Road for 1.5 miles to Sky Oaks Road. Go left on Sky Oaks Road, past the payment kiosk, for 2.1 miles to the parking and picnic area at the base of the dam. GPS: N37 56.977' / W122 35.902'

The Hike

Couple a hike around Lake Lagunitas with a picnic in the shady picnic ground at the base of the dam, and you've got yourself a perfect family outing.

Lake Lagunitas is one of five lakes within the sprawling watershed on the flanks of Mount Tamalpais managed by the Marin Municipal Water District (MMWD). About 110 miles of roads and trails are maintained within the watershed, one of Marin County's most valuable recreational resources. Watershed lands form Marin's backyard, and the Sleeping Lady watches over it all.

The flat, easy loop around Lake Lagunitas, on a wide fire road that invites walking and talking, is very popular. On weekends the picnic area fills and the trail is relatively crowded with hikers, mountain bikers, and horseback riders. Don't let that scare you off: The people-watching is as engaging as the scenery. On weekdays the crowds thin and you will find plenty of space on the trail.

The route begins in the picnic area, where you'll find the remains of a fish hatchery. You can attain the top of the dam via three access routes: Two fire roads flank the dam, and a flight of wood and stone stairs (some of the stone is greenish serpentine) climbs next to the wooden spillway flume. Once atop the dam, take in views of the summits of Mount Tam. Be sure to check the floats for resident turtles sunning themselves. The lake and surrounding watershed support wildlife in abundance, and aside from the turtles you may see deer, songbirds, great blue herons, and possibly otters.

You can hike around the lake in either direction; it is described here counterclockwise. From the dam follow the

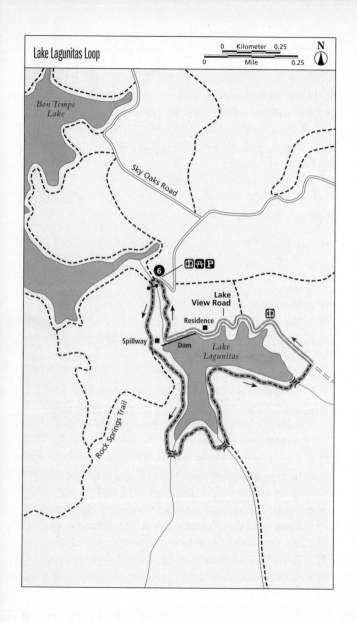

Lake Lagunitas Loop

0   Kilometer   0.25
0   Mile   0.25

N

Bon Tempe
Lake

Sky Oaks Road

6

Lake
View Road

Residence

Spillway   Dam   Lake
Lagunitas

Rock Springs Trail

trail through mixed evergreen forest, with stands of red-woods shading two of the bridges spanning inlet streams. From the southern shore you can look across the lake and up to the green (in winter and spring) or gold (in summer and fall) summit of Pilot Knob. The third bridge is nestled among oaks, and the last leg of the hike, along the Lake View Road, passes through oak woodland and scattered patches of meadow. End the hike back on the dam, retracing your steps back to the trailhead.

Miles and Directions

0.0 Start in the picnic area, climbing to the top of the dam either via the staircase beside the spillway or the fire road that begins at the north end of the picnic ground behind a gate (a bridge spans the creek).

0.15 From the wooden viewing deck, head to the right, walking the loop counterclockwise.

0.25 Pass the junction with the Rock Springs Trail, staying left on the Lagunitas road.

0.5 Cross the first bridge in a redwood grove.

0.6 Cross the second bridge, also in a redwood grove.

1.1 Cross the third bridge, this one among oaks. At the trail junction, go left on the broad dirt Lake View Road (not signed).

1.3 Pass a restroom on the right.

1.4 At the trail junction, stay left on Lake View Road. (FYI: The steep trail to the right leads up to Pilot Knob.)

1.6 Pass a watershed residence, then descend a flight of stone steps to the dam. Cross the dam to the platform and take the stairs back down into the picnic area.

1.7 Arrive back at the trailhead.

7 Point Reyes Lighthouse

Perched on a rocky promontory as far west on the continent as you can go, the historic Point Reyes Lighthouse was a welcome beacon for ships navigating the dangerous coastline. These days it's the beacon at the end of a short trail that, for those who dare, includes a thigh-pumping stair climb.

Distance: 1.2 miles out and back to lighthouse, including the staircase; 1.0 mile out and back to the visitor center and viewing platform

Approximate hiking time: 1 hour

Difficulty: More challenging to the lighthouse; easy to the visitor center

Trail surface: Paved roadway, concrete stairs and ramps

Best seasons: Year-round; spring and fall for the best chance at fog-free days

Other trail users: Occasional park vehicles

Canine compatibility: Dogs not permitted

Fees and permits: No fees or permits required

Schedule: Park trails open daily, sunrise to sunset; lighthouse open 10:00 a.m. to 4:30 p.m.

Thurs through Mon

Trailhead facilities: Small parking lot, limited roadside parking; restrooms. Additional restrooms and information are available at the Lighthouse Visitor Center.

Maps: USGS Drakes Bay; Point Reyes National Seashore map and brochure available at the Bear Valley Visitor Center; map and brochure online at www.nps .gov/pore

Other: The weather can change quickly on the point. Be prepared by wearing clothing suitable for wind, dense fog, and cold.

Trail contacts: Point Reyes National Seashore, 1 Bear Valley Rd., Point Reyes Station, CA 94956; (415) 464-5100; www .nps.gov/pore. The Lighthouse Visitor Center can be reached at (415) 669-1534.

Finding the trailhead: From CA 1 in Point Reyes Station, head south to the Point Reyes National Seashore sign and turn right (west) onto Sir Francis Drake Boulevard. Follow Sir Francis Drake Boulevard for about 20 miles to the road's end at the lighthouse parking lot. GPS: N37 59.868' / W123 00.700'

The Hike

Before the Point Reyes light began flashing its distinctive signal in 1870, shipwrecks were all too frequent along this stretch of northern California's coast. Hidden rocks, turbulent currents, and blindingly dense fogs conspired to make navigation a nightmare off the point, which juts more than 10 miles farther into the Pacific than the rest of the coastline.

Once its foghorn and beautifully faceted Fresnel lens became operational, seamen were able to bring cargo and passengers safely to harbor in San Francisco Bay. The light operated for more than a century before it was shut down in 1975, replaced by an automated light and foghorn housed in a building below the historic structure.

These days the light draws people to the point instead of warning them away. Views from its clifftop perch are amazing. When open, you can tour the lighthouse and associated buildings, taking a walk through seafaring history.

The route to the light begins on the paved access road that leads to the Lighthouse Visitor Center. Pass several interpretive signs and enjoy wonderful views down onto Point Reyes Beach from the gently ascending route. At the halfway point a wind-sculpted bower of cypress arcs over the road. Beyond, you'll cross the driveway for park housing, with a gray whale painted in blue on the asphalt. The visitor center, a little white building anchored in the lee of a large rock outcrop, marks the end of the easy section of

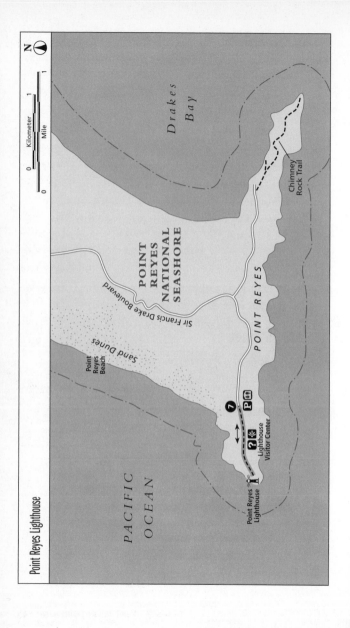

Point Reyes Lighthouse

PACIFIC OCEAN

Point Reyes Beach

Sand Dunes

POINT REYES NATIONAL SEASHORE

Sir Francis Drake Boulevard

Point Reyes Lighthouse

Lighthouse Visitor Center

7

POINT REYES

Drakes Bay

Chimney Rock Trail

N

Kilometer

1

0

1

Mile

the trail. From the observation deck on the west side of the outcrop, you can look down on the squat red-roofed lighthouse and gaze out to sea.

Things get tricky if you decide to tackle the final 0.1 mile down to the light itself—a worthy goal for anyone with nerve and good knees. Negotiate the 308 stairs and a couple of steep concrete ramps, and the mission is accomplished. It's not as daunting as it looks: Take your time, use the rest stops along the way, and you'll make it out and back no problem.

Options: Point Reyes National Seashore brims with spectacular hiking trails. Pair the lighthouse walk with a wildflower walk at Chimney Rock in spring—massively popular with those who know and love Point Reyes—or journey to Bear Valley and walk the interpretive Earthquake Trail. Pick up a park map for more options.

Miles and Directions

- **0.0** Start by passing the gate onto the paved road. Dirt side trails lead to overlooks and interpretive signs on the right.
- **0.3** Cypress trees hover over the trail, framing views of Point Reyes Beach.
- **0.5** Arrive at the Lighthouse Visitor Center. A large cement cistern is on the left. Follow the path past the whale skull and interpretive signs to the viewing platform. The descent to the lighthouse begins here.
- **0.6** Arrive at the lighthouse. Check out the views and buildings, then climb back to the viewing platform thirty stories above.
- **1.2** Arrive back at the trailhead.

8 Abbotts Lagoon

A chorus of chirping songbirds and lowing dairy cows accompanies hikers along the trail to Abbotts Lagoon, which spans fields of lush wildflower–studded scrub and ends amid windswept dunes at the edge of the turbulent Pacific.

Distance: 3.0 miles out and back

Approximate hiking time: 1.5 hours

Difficulty: Easy

Trail surface: Dirt singletrack, sand

Best seasons: Year-round; wildflower display best in spring

Other trail users: Bird watchers

Canine compatibility: Dogs not permitted

Fees and permits: No fees or permits required

Schedule: Open daily, sunrise to sunset

Trailhead facilities: Ample parking; restrooms, trashcans, interpretive signs

Maps: USGS Drakes Bay; Point Reyes National Seashore map and brochure available at the Bear Valley Visitor Center; map and brochure online at www.nps .gov/pore

Special considerations: Please respect seasonal closure of the dunes to protect nesting western snowy plovers. Do not swim or wade at Point Reyes Beach; surf and currents are dangerous.

Trail contacts: Point Reyes National Seashore, 1 Bear Valley Rd., Point Reyes Station, CA 94956; (415) 464-5100; www .nps.gov/pore

Finding the trailhead: From CA 1 in Point Reyes Station, head south to the Point Reyes National Seashore sign and turn right (west) onto Sir Francis Drake Boulevard. Travel 6.4 miles on Sir Francis Drake to Pierce Point Road and turn right (north). Follow Pierce Point Road for 3.4 miles to the signed Abbotts Lagoon trailhead on the left (west). GPS: N38 07.411' / W122 56.132'.

The Hike

I've done a little hiking in my day, traveling miles through some of the loveliest terrain in North America, including Yosemite, the Colorado Rockies, Alaska, and the Yukon. But here's the truth: If I could hike only one trail, I would head out to Abbotts Lagoon. The water, the wildflowers, the weather, the dunes, the birds, even the cows—they've conspired to enchant me, no matter the season. I've no doubt you'll agree. It may not become your favorite, but it is a superlative day hike.

The springtime wildflower display is not to be missed. Fields of orange fiddleneck and poppy, mounds of purple iris, beach blankets of yellow and purple lupine, expanses of windblown wild radish, and that just grazes the surface of what grows here.

Speaking of grazing, the dairy cows that mow ranchland on the other side of the fence play a role in making the wildflower display even more spectacular: The juxtaposition of their uniformly cropped pasture with the random colors and textures of the scrub is impossible to overlook.

Then there are the birds, which are endlessly engaging. You're likely to see perky white-crowned sparrows, jittery California quail, flirting red-winged blackbirds, and stately great blue herons, along with the more ubiquitous gulls, crows, and turkey vultures. But the stars are the protected western snowy plovers. During the nesting season the National Park Service fences off the dunes where the plovers tend their eggs, creating an unusual sight in an overused park—waves of sand untouched by human footprints.

The relatively flat trail is easy to follow—a gravel-and-dirt singletrack winding down to a bridge that spans the

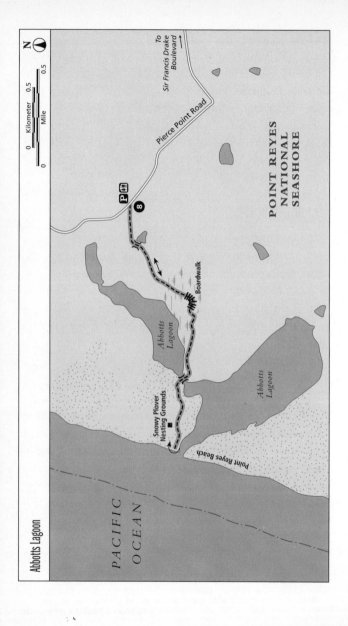

Abbotts Lagoon

PACIFIC
OCEAN

Point Reyes Beach

Snowy Plover
Nesting Grounds

Abbotts
Lagoon

Abbotts Lagoon

Boardwalk

POINT REYES
NATIONAL SEASHORE

Pierce Point Road

To
Sir Francis Drake
Boulevard

N

0   Kilometer   0.5

0   Mile   0.5

isthmus between the outer and inner lagoons. A raised boardwalk helps keep your feet dry and protects delicate plants and wildlife in a marshy zone. Once across the bridge, the trail disappears in the shifting sands. Follow the edge of the outer lagoon out to the northern reaches of Point Reyes Beach, where the Pacific curls forcefully onto land. By contrast, the water in the sprawling lagoon, rippled by ocean breezes, licks the sand gently, inviting the wading that the surf precludes.

Miles and Directions

0.0 Start by dropping gently downhill on the gravel path.

0.2 Pass a bench, cross a small bridge, and skirt a small pond.

0.4 Pass a bench and an interpretive sign on the ecology of coastal dunes.

0.6 Cross the boardwalk that protects the marshy area. The gravel gives way to a dirt surface as the trail follows a fence-line.

1.0 Crest a rise, then drop to the bridge over the narrow inlet between the two arms of the lagoon. A social trail climbs the hill to the left. Cross the bridge and continue toward the beach on the best-trod trail in the sand. The tide will dictate the route, but follow the north shore of the lagoon to the beach.

1.5 Reach the beach. Take in the views, then retrace your steps.

3.0 Arrive back at the trailhead.

Sonoma County

9 Lower Tubbs Island Trail

A long, contemplative hike along ranch roads and levee tops leads through the marshlands along Sonoma County's San Pablo Bay coastline. Expect excellent birding and solitude, especially along the loop on Lower Tubbs Island itself.

Distance: 8.2-mile lollipop
Approximate hiking time: 4 hours
Difficulty: More challenging due to trail length
Trail surface: Ranch road, levee tops
Best seasons: Year-round; muddy trail surfaces during and following rainstorms and high tides
Other trail users: Bird watchers; occasional cars and trucks on ranch roads
Canine compatibility: Dogs not permitted
Fees and permits: No fees or permits required
Schedule: Open daily, sunrise to sunset

Trailhead facilities: Large dirt parking lot; information signboard, trashcans
Maps: USGS Sears Point and Petaluma Point; maps posted on information signboards; map and brochure online at www.fws.gov/ sfbayrefuges/San%20Pablo/ San%20Pablo%20Gen.pdf
Special considerations: Waterfowl hunting is permitted from October to January. Contact the sanctuary office for more information.
Trail contacts: San Pablo Bay National Wildlife Refuge, 7715 Lakeville Hwy., Petaluma, CA 94954; (707) 769-4200; www .fws.gov/sfbayrefuges/San%20 Pablo

Finding the trailhead: From the junction of CA 37 and CA 121 at Sears Point, follow CA 37 for 0.7 mile east (toward Vallejo). The signed trailhead and parking lot are on the right (south) side of the highway. **Note:** You cannot turn left (west) from the trailhead lot. Exit to the east, following CA 37 to a safe turnaround spot. GPS: N38 09.184' / W122 26.169'.

The Hike

Once upon a time, extensive estuaries and wetlands surrounded San Francisco Bay. Then came the gold rush, and sediments from mining operations washed down the Sacramento and San Joaquin Rivers, filling in the shallow tidal marshes. Then came rapid development of the Bay Area, and more wetlands were filled in to create new land for housing and industry.

It wasn't until more than 75 percent of San Francisco Bay's wetlands and tidal marshes were gone that environmentalists and government agencies, recognizing the value of the marshes to wildlife and the health of the bay, began to work toward their preservation.

The wetlands of northern San Pablo Bay are part of this ongoing multiagency reclamation and preservation effort. Currently two large parcels have been preserved as part of the San Pablo Bay National Wildlife Refuge—the Lower Tubbs Island Unit off Sears Point and the Cullinan Ranch Unit near Mare Island—and conservationists hope to ultimately preserve more than 20,000 acres.

Depending on the season, hikers can view a variety of plant and animal life along the trail. More than 300 wildlife species either live in or pass through the tidal preserve. Birds are a huge draw: The refuge attracts seabirds and shorebirds galore, including ducks, pelicans, gulls, plovers, and sandpipers. Songbirds and raptors (including northern harriers and white-tailed kites) also nest and hunt in the marshes. Bring a guidebook: Chances are you'll see or hear things you've never seen or heard before. Seals, butterflies, rodents, and rabbits may also be encountered along the route. Pickleweed and salt grasses dominate the vegetation, but colorful wildflowers crowd the path in spring.

The lollipop loop begins by following Tolay Creek, which empties into San Pablo Bay at Lower Tubbs Island. Follow levee tops and ranch roads out toward the bay—the refuge is bordered by ranchland, so you may encounter truck and car traffic on the "stick" portion of the lollipop. Highway noise, along with the occasional power whine of a race car at nearby Infineon Raceway, is also present. But on the "pop" portion of the hike, it's just you and the birds. The views don't quit: Both stick and pop feature panoramic vistas of Bay Area landmarks, including Mount Tamalpais, the Richmond–San Rafael Bridge, the East Bay hills, Mount Diablo, and the Carquinez Strait. On a clear day you can see the San Francisco skyline.

You can travel the loop in either direction; it's described here counterclockwise, heading right from the island trail junction. Bridges span tidal channels along the first leg of the loop, and bay waters lap the shoreline on its outer reaches. Close the loop at the refuge interpretive sign and retrace your steps to the trailhead.

Miles and Directions

0.0 Start by passing the gate and heading down the dirt ranch road. The information signboard at the trailhead labels this the Napa-Sonoma Marshes Wildlife Area Tolay Creek Unit.

0.3 The trail bends south after circling the Upper Tolay Lagoon; pass a sign for the San Pablo Bay National Wildlife Refuge. The levee top and ranch road run parallel; take the high road for better views.

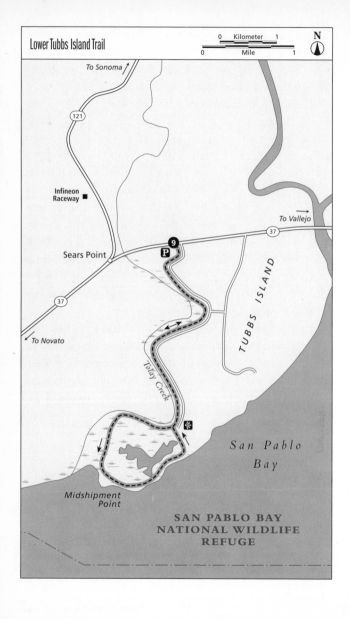

Lower Tubbs Island Trail

To Sonoma

121

Infineon
Raceway

To Vallejo

37

Sears Point

9
P

TUBBS ISLAND

To Novato

37

Tolay Creek

San Pablo
Bay

Midshipment
Point

SAN PABLO BAY
NATIONAL WILDLIFE
REFUGE

0   Kilometer   1
0   Mile   1

N

1.0 The ranch road splits. Go right, following small white-and-blue refuge signs on the levee top.

1.8 The levee and road bear left (south), passing a sheet-metal pumphouse. Again, the best views are from the levee top.

2.7 Arrive at the lower island. The trail splits; go right, past interpretive signs, on the sometimes eroded, sometimes weedy, elevated trailbed. Red ranch buildings are ahead.

3.4 The trail arcs southwest and crosses the first bridge over a tidal channel.

3.6 Cross the second bridge and tidal channel.

3.8 Pass a bench overlooking the wetlands.

4.0 Reach the bayshore. The trail bends east. Little shoreline beaches offer great places to take in the views.

4.4 Pass a dilapidated tidal floodgate.

5.2 Pass a second floodgate, then the trail curves sharply north.

5.5 Close the loop. Turn right and retrace your steps.

8.2 Arrive back at the trailhead.

10 Ridge and Panorama Trails Loop (Helen Putnam Regional Park)

Tucked in the rolling hills along the Sonoma-Marin county line, this loop climbs through grasslands to an oak-studded ridgeline with great views across west county ranchlands and east across Petaluma to Sonoma Mountain.

Distance: 1.5-mile loop
Approximate hiking time: 1.5 hours
Difficulty: More challenging due to elevation change and a steep descent on the Panorama Trail
Trail surface: Dirt singletrack, pavement, ranch road
Best seasons: Year-round; rain may make trails muddy and slick
Other trail users: Mountain bikers, equestrians
Canine compatibility: Leashed dogs permitted
Fees and permits: Parking fee

Schedule: Open daily, sunrise to sunset
Trailhead facilities: Ample parking, equestrian parking; restrooms, picnic sites, a tot lot, trashcans, water
Maps: USGS Petaluma; trail map on information kiosk at the trailhead; online at www.sonoma countyparks.org
Trail contacts: County of Sonoma Regional Parks Department, 2300 County Center Dr., Suite 120A, Santa Rosa, CA 95403; (707) 565-2041; www .sonomacounty.org/parks

Finding the trailhead: From US 101 in Petaluma, take the Washington Street exit. Follow Washington Street for 1.1 miles west to Petaluma Boulevard North and turn left. Follow Petaluma Boulevard for 0.1 mile to Western Avenue and turn right (west). Follow Western Avenue for 2 miles to Chileno Valley Road and turn left. Follow Chileno Valley Road for 0.8 mile to the trailhead parking lot on the left. GPS: N38 12.770' / W122 39.833'

The Hike

A lovely bowl filled with meadow grasses and wildflowers crowns this trail loop. A local favorite that's well worth a visit for out-of-towners, the route skirts a small pond on the way up and features wonderful views of both the Petaluma River valley to the east and west county ranchland to the west.

Begin by picking up the dirt Ridge Trail; the paved ranch road below shares the name and parallels the single-track, passing two private residences. The dirt track meets the paved at Fish Pond, where you continue uphill on the pavement. Views back down valley are worth pausing for as you climb.

The pavement ends at a trail junction bordering a huge bowl filled with meadow grasses and wildflowers. In the rainy season the grasses green up; come warmer weather, the wildflowers bust out—poppies, lupines, fiddlenecks, iris, paintbrush, and more. As summer progresses into fall, the grasses burn gold, with oak groves providing pockets of greenery and shade. Turkey vultures, hawks, and kites ride the air currents rising from the bowl, circling easily as they scan the grassland for prey.

Pick up the Panorama Trail and climb to the bench where "Donna said yes" (according to the plaque). Views spread east to Sonoma Mountain and west over the ranch-lands, and to the south you can peek through the hills to the bay and Mount Diablo.

Cruise the ridgetop, passing junctions with the Savannah, Arroyo, and Pomo Trails. Spreading oaks with multiple trunks form bowers of leafy shade as you descend, their boughs reaching down to kiss the grass. Traverse a second,

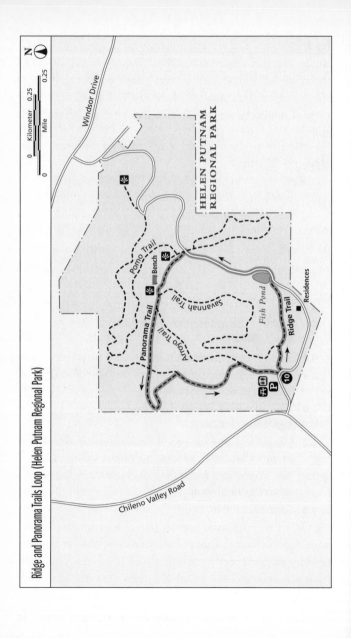

Ridge and Panorama Trails Loop (Helen Putnam Regional Park)

N

Kilometer 0.25
Mile 0.25

Windsor Drive

HELEN PUTNAM
REGIONAL PARK

Pomo Trail

Bench

Panorama Trail

Savannah Trail

Arroyo Trail

Fish Pond

Ridge Trail

Residences

P

10

Chileno Valley Road

steeper bowl to a second junction with the Pomo Trail. Enjoy the views a last time, then plunge steeply down to the trailhead. The descent can be tough on knees, but it is short and can be managed more easily if you create your own switchbacks across the broad dirt track. Watch your step, and feel the burn.

Miles and Directions

0.0 Begin on the signed singletrack Ridge Trail, which parallels the paved trail.

0.1 Pass the junction with the Savannah Trail, staying right and uphill on the Ridge Trail.

0.3 Pass the Cattail Trail junction; continue up past the water tank to the edge of the pond. Go right over the dam to the pavement and then left to continue on the Ridge Trail.

0.6 At the junction in the bowl where the Panorama, Pomo, Ridge, and South Loop Trails meet, go left on the signed Panorama Trail.

0.7 Reach the overlook bench.

0.8 Pass the top of the Savannah Trail, then the Arroyo Trail, staying right at both junctions.

1.0 Pass the Pomo Trail intersection, staying straight on the signed Panorama Trail.

1.2 Traverse a steep grassy bowl to a second junction with the Pomo Trail. Go right (southwest) on the Panorama Trail.

1.3 Pass another overlook bench before beginning the steep descent to the trailhead.

1.5 Arrive back at the trailhead.

11 Sonoma Overlook Trail

Take a seat on any of the stone benches at the summit of this route and bask in stunning vistas across the Sonoma Valley. On the descent, check out historic gravestones in the Mountain Cemetery.

Distance: 2.5-mile lollipop

Approximate hiking time: 1 hour

Difficulty: Moderate due to elevation change

Trail surface: Dirt singletrack, paved cemetery roads

Best seasons: Year-round; trail may be muddy in places during and after rainstorms

Other trail users: Trail runners

Canine compatibility: Dogs not permitted

Fees and permits: No fees or permits required

Schedule: Open daily, sunrise to sunset

Trailhead facilities: Small ten-car parking area; picnic table, water, trashcans, information kiosk with interpretive materials; restrooms located behind the mausoleum in the cemetery

Maps: USGS Sonoma; map in the interpretive brochure available at trailhead kiosk

Trail contacts: Sonoma Overlook Trail/Sonoma Ecology Center, P.O. Box 533, Sonoma, CA 95476; www.sonomaecology center.org

Finding the trailhead: From the junction of Broadway and Napa Street (CA 12) in downtown Sonoma at the plaza, go west 1 block to First Street West. Turn right (north) on First Street West and go 0.5 mile to the Mountain Cemetery and signed trailhead on the right. GPS: N38 17.979' / W122 27.430'

The Hike

Ascending a hillside behind Sonoma's historic plaza, the Sonoma Overlook Trail showcases the city's natural and human history, from springtime wildflowers and shady oak and bay laurel groves to the tiered gravesites of some of its founding families.

And then there are the views. On a clear day you can gaze south over the Sonoma Valley to San Pablo Bay and beyond. Sprawling Sonoma Mountain dominates the western horizon.

The overlook trail begins at the entrance to the historic Mountain Cemetery. Follow the gently climbing singletrack through riparian habitat to a creek crossing. Keep an eye out for discreet placards that identify native plants. Beyond the creek, a series of easy switchbacks and long traverses lead up Shocken Hill, passing stone memorial benches along the way.

The path to the Toyon trailhead in the Mountain Cemetery breaks right about midway through the climb. Ignore it on the ascent, staying left and uphill; you'll take this on the descent.

A final rocky stretch leads to the junction with the Upper Meadow Loop. You can hike the 0.3-mile loop in either direction, but it's described here clockwise, climbing past stone benches dedicated to lovers of Sonoma's wildlands. Lichen-stained rocks jut from the grasses, which are vibrant with wildflowers in spring—lupine, poppy, blue-eyed grass, sticky monkey flower, vetch, fiddleneck, clover, and more. Coyote brush crowds the trail at the top of the loop, but you won't be without views for long. As the loop begins its descent, an interpretive sign identifies the peaks spread on the horizon, from Rocky Ridge to Mount Tamalpais.

Close the loop and retrace your steps to the Toyon junction, dropping left to the Mountain Cemetery boundary. Pass the graves of the Rose family as you reach paved

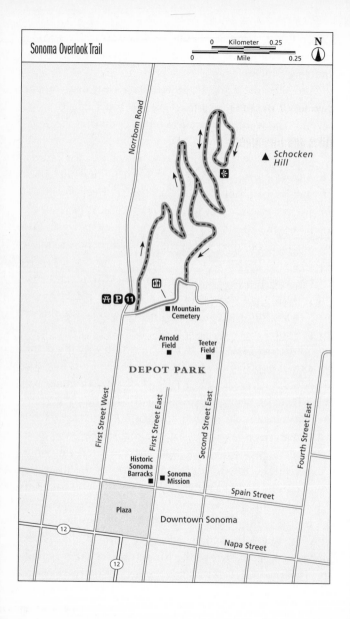

Sonoma Overlook Trail

0   Kilometer   0.25

0   Mile   0.25

N

Norrbom Road

▲ Schocken Hill

🗻

🖾 P ⑪

🚻

■ Mountain Cemetery

Arnold Field ■

Teeter Field ■

DEPOT PARK

First Street West

First Street East

Second Street East

Fourth Street East

Historic Sonoma Barracks ■

■ Sonoma Mission

Spain Street

Plaza

Downtown Sonoma

⑫

Napa Street

⑫

Toyon Road, then follow quiet cemetery lanes down to the entrance gates and the trailhead. Keep an eye out for names you might recognize among the stones: General Mariano Vallejo is buried here, along with Henry Ernest Boyes, founder of Boyes Hot Springs, and others.

Miles and Directions

0.0 Start by climbing the singletrack trail behind the information signboard.

0.2 Cross the streamlet and begin the easy, switchbacking ascent.

0.3 Catch a preview of the summit views and pass a stone memorial bench dedicated to Gypsy Bob.

0.7 Pass the path to the Toyon trailhead, staying left (straight) on the ascending path.

1.1 Arrive at the junction with the Upper Meadow Loop. Go left (clockwise), passing a series of stone viewing benches.

1.4 Close the loop; turn left and retrace your steps to the Toyon trailhead junction.

1.8 Go left on the path to the Toyon trailhead.

2.0 Reach the Mountain Cemetery boundary. Turn right on Toyon Road and follow cemetery roads down to the base of the hill.

2.5 Pass the cemetery gates and arrive back at the trailhead.

12 Wolf House and Lake Trails (Jack London State Historic Park)

This tour of historic sites in Glen Ellen's premier hiking destination includes the ruins of the author's dream home and the man-made lake where Jack and his guests cooled off on hot summer afternoons.

Distance: 3.6 miles out and back

Approximate hiking time: 2 hours

Difficulty: Moderate due to the climb to London Lake

Trail surface: Patches of pavement; dirt ranch road, singletrack

Best seasons: Year-round

Other trail users: Mountain bikers and equestrians on the dirt road to London Lake

Canine compatibility: No dogs permitted

Fees and permits: Day-use fee

Schedule: Open year-round from 10:00 a.m. to 5:00 p.m. daily

Trailhead facilities: Ample parking; restrooms, trashcans, water, picnic tables, information signboard with a park trail map

Maps: USGS Glen Ellen; maps posted at trailhead kiosks; maps and brochures available at the House of Happy Walls; online at www.parks.ca.gov

Other: The museum and gift shop in the House of Happy Walls is open from 10:00 a.m. to 5:00 p.m. daily except on Thanksgiving, Christmas, and New Year's Day. Interpretive information is available through the Valley of the Moon Natural History Association (www.jack londonpark.com).

Special considerations: No swimming is permitted in London Lake.

Trail contacts: Jack London State Historic Park, 2400 London Ranch Rd., Glen Ellen, CA 95442; (707) 938-5216; www .parks.ca.gov

Finding the trailhead: From the stoplight at Arnold Drive and Sonoma Highway (CA 12), signed for Glen Ellen, take Arnold Drive west for 1 mile to its intersection with London Ranch Road. Turn right (west) onto London Ranch Road and go about 1.5 miles to the entrance kiosk. The trailhead is in the lower parking lot to the left. GPS: N32 21.389' / W122 32.520'

The Hike

Jack London's *Call of the Wild* is a staple of libraries and middle school English classes. Likewise, a tour of London's Beauty Ranch is a staple of the Sonoma County hiking scene.

London's ranch is set between the foot of Sonoma Mountain and quaint Glen Ellen, a little village with more than its share of fine restaurants and family wineries. London established the ranch at the turn of the twentieth century, building first a cottage that he shared with his wife, Charmian, and then a stone-walled mansion that would succumb to fire before he could occupy it.

This tour of Jack London State Historic Park takes you first to the House of Happy Walls, Charmian's home following the death of her husband. Next is the author's grave: He lies in an oak-shaded glen with his wife and, in a separate plot, the two children of homesteaders who came before him, David and Lilly Greenlaw.

A short hitch over a meadowy knoll drops into the redwood grove surrounding the ruins of the Wolf House. A trail circling the reinforced stone walls features information signboards that include architectural plans and a viewing platform offering a second-story view from the end of the empty reflecting pool.

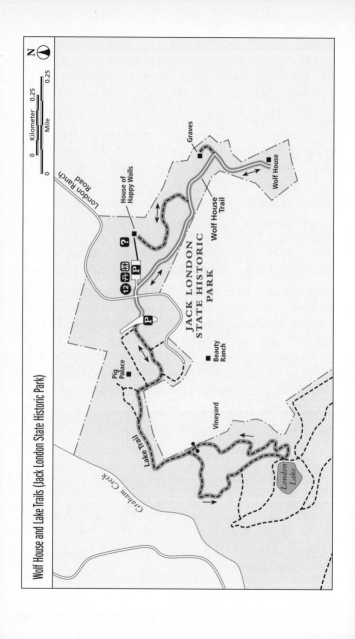

Wolf House and Lake Trails (Jack London State Historic Park)

The second leg of the hike, on the Lake Trail, leads through historic ranch buildings, an operating vineyard, and up to London Lake. The route climbs through a eucalyptus-shaded picnic ground, then down past stone barns, a cactus garden, and the London cottage, which is open for tours. Circle the vineyard, passing the footpath to the Pig Palace, to the trail junction on the west side of the vineyard at a gate. Go right and up on the singletrack, hikers-only Lake Trail, climbing switchbacks through redwoods and mixed evergreen forest to London Lake.

Over the years the lake has filled with silt, and its arcing stone dam is leaky and in need of repair. The Jack London Lake Alliance (www.jacklondonlake.org) is working to rehabilitate the lake. In the meantime it presents a pleasing place for a picnic and supports a population of songbirds and ducks.

From the lake, follow the service road back to the gate, then retrace your steps to the trailhead.

Options: Other great park routes include the Mountain Trail, which leads to the summit of Sonoma Mountain and is well worth the 8.0-mile round-trip trek for experienced hikers. Additional trails lead to an old orchard and a grand old redwood known locally as the Grandmother Tree. Consult a trail map for options.

Miles and Directions

0.0 Start by following the paved path for about 500 feet to the House of Happy Walls and the signed trail to the Wolf House. Drop down the singletrack Wolf House Trail.

0.4 Meet the paved Wolf House Service Road at a bench and water fountain. Go left (east).

0.5 At the signed trail Y, go left on the singletrack path to Jack London's gravesite.

0.6 Arrive at the graves. Retrace your steps to the service road and go left toward the Wolf House.

0.8 Arrive at the Wolf House. Circle the ruins, then retrace your steps to the junction with the trail to the House of Happy Walls.

1.2 At the Happy Walls trail junction, continue straight on the service road.

1.5 Arrive at the gated end of the ranch road. Cross the parking lot, then London Ranch Road, and climb through the upper parking lot to the signed Lake Trail.

1.6 Arrive at the gravel Lake Trail and follow it through the ranch, passing the barns, cottage, silos, and Pig Palace. The road follows the fenced boundary of the vineyard.

2.2 A gate spans the trail at the junction on the west side of the vineyard. Turn right and follow the hikers-only Lake Trail.

2.5 Pass a closed trail, staying straight on the Lake Trail.

2.6 Rejoin the ranch road (the Lake Service Road) and complete the final bit of uphill to the lake. Explore the shoreline and dam, then follow the service road down to the gate at the trail junction. Stay straight on the dirt road, retracing your steps to the trailhead.

3.6 Arrive back at the trailhead.

13 Planet Walk and Creekside Nature Trails (Sugarloaf Ridge State Park)

Experience space travel with your feet firmly planted on Earth on the Planet Walk. Trailside interpretive signs mark the relative distances between the planets in the solar system. A more traditional nature trail leads to the Planet Walk.

Distance: 3.5-mile lollipop

Approximate hiking time: 2 hours

Difficulty: Moderate due to distance and elevation changes

Trail surface: Dirt singletrack, dirt doubletrack

Best seasons: Spring and fall

Other trail users: Mountain bikers and equestrians on the Meadow and Hillside Trails

Canine compatibility: No dogs permitted

Fees and permits: Entrance fee

Schedule: Open daily, 8:00 a.m. to sunset

Trailhead facilities: Large dirt parking area; restrooms, trashcans, camping, water, and a visitor center located nearby

Maps: USGS Kenwood and Rutherford; trail map and brochure available at the entrance kiosk for a fee; map on information signboard; online at www.parks.ca.gov

Other: The park's visitor center offers interpretive guides and exhibits about the area's natural history. The Ferguson Observatory is open for public solar and night sky viewing; visit www.rfo.org or call (707) 833-6979. Guided trail rides are provided by Triple Creek Horse Outfit (www.triplecreekhorseoutfit.com; 707-887-8700).

Trail contacts: Sugarloaf Ridge State Park, 2605 Adobe Canyon Road, Kenwood, CA 95452; (707) 833-5712; www.parks.ca.gov

Finding the trailhead: From the junction of Sonoma Highway (CA 12) and Adobe Canyon Road in Kenwood, go east on Adobe Canyon Road. Drive 3.4 miles to the entrance kiosk. The road actually does continue, but is not open to the public (except for special events). The trailhead parking area is just beyond the kiosk on the left (north). GPS: N38 26.276' / W122 30.876'

The Hike

Onetime home to the native Wappo people, and later to ranchers and farmers, the mountainous terrain now known as Sugarloaf Ridge State Park hosts a variety of recreational and educational pursuits. You can camp, take a trail ride, view the stars at the Ferguson Observatory . . . and hike from the Sun to Pluto.

Sugarloaf straddles the Mayacamas Mountains, which divide Sonoma and Napa Counties. Its high point, Bald Mountain, offers great views, and seasonal streams flowing out of the steep ravines converge to form the headwaters of Sonoma Creek. Meadows bloom with wildflowers in spring and early summer, and fragrant oak woodlands offer shade and habitat for a variety of plants and critters.

All good stuff, but where else can you traverse a million miles of space in a single step?

The Planet Walk begins in the parking lot of the Ferguson Observatory and within the first hundred feet or so passes most of the inner planets (marked with interpretive signs that describe their relative sizes and distances from the Sun). Mars lies a bit down the Meadow Trail, and from there the planets are separated by space that, in this case, is filled with meadow grasses and stands of oak. Each step you take equals one million miles, and if you take a step every five seconds, you're traveling at the speed of light. The solar system has been scaled down more than two billion times to fit within the confines of the park, but Neptune and poor demoted Pluto are too far out there to be included in this easy hike. You'll go as far as Uranus before heading back to Earth.

The loop described here begins and ends on the Creekside Nature Trail. The interpretive guide to the trail, included with the park brochure, describes the plants that thrive along the course of Sonoma Creek, as well as their uses. The Planet Walk and Creekside Nature Trail are linked by the Hillside Trail, a roller-coaster ramble overlooking the western highlands of the park.

The Planet Walk and Hillside Trail loop can be hiked in either direction, but to begin at the Sun and end at Uranus, it is described in a clockwise direction.

Miles and Directions

0.0 Start by crossing the park road to the start of the Creekside Nature Trail. Pass a picnic site and a side trail leading across the creek to the campground.

0.1 Reach the amphitheater. Cross the campground access trail and continue on the nature trail (a post with a leaf sign marks the path).

0.4 At interpretive post #12, cross the bridge over the creek.

0.5 At the trail junction, go left and downhill on the Hillside Trail. The creek must be forded in winter and spring but may be dry in late summer and fall.

0.8 The Hillside Trail continues past the stables to meet the Meadow Trail. The Ferguson Observatory and the start of the Planet Walk are to the left, behind the gate. Locate the Sun on the left (west) side of the observatory parking lot. Mercury is opposite, Venus is 149 feet (or sixty-seven

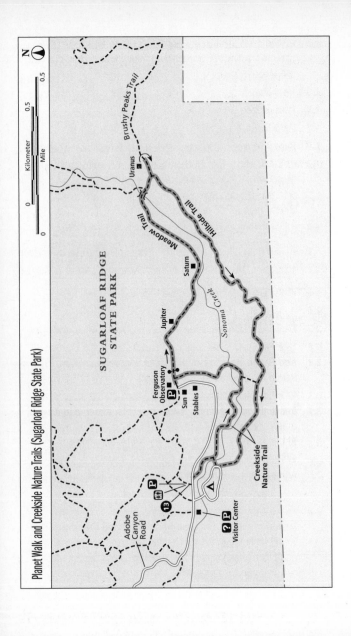

Planet Walk and Creekside Nature Trails (Sugarloaf Ridge State Park)

SUGARLOAF RIDGE
STATE PARK

Brushy Peaks Trail

Uranus

Meadow Trail

Hillside Trail

Saturn

Sonoma Creek

Jupiter

Ferguson
Observatory

Sun

Stables

Creekside Nature Trail

Adobe
Canyon Road

Visitor Center

N

Kilometer   0.5

Mile   0.5

million miles) to the north, and Earth is on the observatory wall. To reach Mars, backtrack to the gate and head out on the Meadow Trail.

1.0 Pass Mars.

1.1 Pass Jupiter.

1.3 Pass Saturn.

1.6 Pass a picnic site and cross the bridge over Sonoma Creek.

1.7 At the junction with the Gray Pine Trail, stay right on the Meadow Trail. Climb about 100 yards to the intersection with the Hillside and Brushy Peaks Trails. Go left, up the Brushy Peaks Trail, toward Uranus.

1.8 Arrive at Uranus and the turnaround point on the Planet Walk. (FYI: Neptune lies about 1.0 mile farther, with Pluto beyond.) Retrace your steps to the Hillside/Meadow Trail junction.

1.9 At the junction, turn left on the Hillside Trail.

2.5 A steep pitch climbs past power poles.

2.7 Descend past water tanks to a picnic table, bench, and viewpoint.

2.9 Arrive at an intersection with the Creekside Nature Trail. Go left on the nature trail, passing posts #16 and #17 before crossing the creek.

3.1 Reach the campground. Follow the campground road down to the restrooms (at Campsite 15) and pick up the trail link to the amphitheater. From the amphitheater, retrace your steps to the trailhead.

3.5 Arrive back at the trailhead.

14 Spring Lake

Without question one of the most well-used, well-loved trails in Sonoma County, this accessible, mostly paved route begins in busy Howarth Park and circumnavigates Spring Lake, a pretty little reservoir.

Distance: 3.6-mile lollipop
Approximate hiking time: 2 hours
Difficulty: Moderate due to trail length
Trail surface: Paved; 0.5-mile gravel section
Best seasons: Year-round
Other trail users: Cyclists, joggers (equestrians on specified dirt trails only)
Canine compatibility: Leashed dogs permitted
Fees and permits: No fee charged at the Howarth Park entrance; fee at the Spring Lake Regional Park entrances on Violetti Road and Newanga Avenue
Schedule: Open daily, sunrise to sunset
Trailhead facilities: Large parking lot; restrooms, water, trashcans, trail map and information signboard, amusement park concessions

Maps: USGS Santa Rosa; map on information board at trailhead; online at ci.santa-rosa .ca.us/doclib/Documents/ Howarth%20Park%20Trail%20 Map.pdf
Other: The parking lots fill quickly on weekends. Visit on weekdays to avoid crowds. Amusement park rides and concessions, boat rentals, campgrounds, and the Spring Lake swimming lagoon are open seasonally; contact the park for more information.
Trail contacts: Howarth Park, c/o City of Santa Rosa Department of Recreation, Parks, and Community Services, Steele Lane Community Center, 415 Steele Lane, Santa Rosa, CA 95403; (707) 543-3298; ci.santa-rosa .ca.us/departments/recreation andparks/programs/howarth park. Spring Lake Regional Park, County of Sonoma Regional Parks Department, 2300

County Center Dr., Suite 120A, Santa Rosa, CA 95403; (707) 539-8092; www.sonoma-county.org/parks/pk_slake.htm.

Finding the trailhead: From US 101 in Santa Rosa, take the CA 12 exit and head east on CA 12 toward Sonoma. The freeway ends at Farmers Lane. Stay straight through the traffic light, crossing Farmers Lane, onto Hoen Avenue. Follow Hoen Avenue for 1.5 miles to Summerfield Road. Turn left (north) onto Summerfield Road and go 0.7 mile to the signed entrance to Howarth Park on the right, at 630 Summerfield Rd. Follow the park road to the upper parking lot. GPS: N38 27.208' / W122 40.065'

The Hike

A ramble through Howarth Park and around Spring Lake leads from a playland frequented by little people to a reservoir frequented by geese and ducks. On any given day you'll share the paved path with a kaleidoscope of dog walkers, moms jogging with babes in strollers, anglers, couples of all ages strolling hand in hand, and cross-country teams from local schools.

Though several trailheads exist, this route begins in Howarth Park, adjacent to Lake Ralphine. Other Howarth Park attractions include a tot lot, tennis courts, a rock climbing wall, and the small amusement park with a miniature train, merry-go-round, and pony rides. An information signboard with trail map is at the trailhead.

The trail climbs through dense oak woodland toward neighboring Spring Lake Regional Park. Dirt tracks lead right and left off the paved path, and trailside benches offer chances for rest and people-watching. Crest a short, steep rise (the top of West Saddle Dam); turn left and drop to the circle path around Spring Lake. You can walk the loop

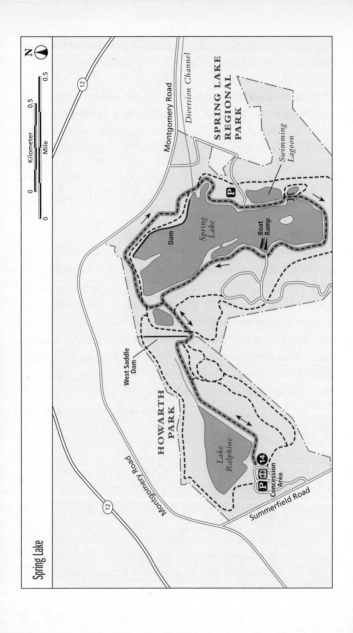

Spring Lake

in either direction, but it is described here clockwise (turn left). Take advantage of the par course installations if you want to firm and tone more than your legs.

The lake is out of sight at first, coming into view as you climb onto the long dam on the north side. Dropping off the dam, follow the path across the Channel Drive side trail and the Santa Rosa Creek diversion channel. Circle to the Spring Lake concession area, where in summer you'll find boat rentals, a snack bar, showers, restrooms, and the swimming lagoon. Over the bridge you'll find the Children's Memorial Garden and Oak Knoll picnic ground, which borders Annadel State Park.

At the next parking area, on the west shore of the lake, a boat launch slides into the water. Stay lakeside, picking up the wide, dirt Fisherman's Trail for the last 0.5 mile of the loop. Hitch up with the paved path again, and head left to retrace your steps to the trailhead.

Options: Neighboring Annadel State Park contains miles of dirt roads and singletrack trails that are immensely popular with local mountain bikers. If you're willing to share the trails, there is plenty of fine terrain to be explored. More information and maps of Annadel trails are available at www.parks.ca.gov.

Miles and Directions

0.0 Start at the signed Howarth Park trailhead.

0.1 At the junction go left on the pavement, with Lake Ralphine on the left.

0.6 Reach the top of West Saddle Dam. Turn left and drop into the Spring Lake basin.

0.7 At the three-way junction, stay left on the paved path, circling the lake clockwise.

1.1 Reach the top of the main dam.

1.3 Turn right and drop off the dam. Back at lakeside, cross the Channel Drive access trail and the Santa Rosa Creek diversion channel.

1.5 Arrive at the parking lot for the Spring Lake concession area. The path passes between the lakeshore and the swimming lagoon.

1.9 At the south end of the lagoon stay right, crossing the bridge over the Spring Lake diversion channel, then stay right again. (FYI: Trails to the left lead into the children's garden, the Oak Knoll group picnic area, and Annadel State Park.) Continue circling the lake.

2.3 Arrive at the boat launch area. Stay lakeside, joining the dirt Fisherman's Trail. An information signboard marks the path.

2.9 Return to the paved trail below the West Saddle Dam. Turn left to retrace your steps, going right at the crest of the dam to drop back into Howarth Park.

3.6 Arrive back at the trailhead.

15 East Ridge and Pioneer Trails (Armstrong Redwoods State Natural Reserve)

Stretch your legs on a steady climb to the ridgetop overlooking Armstrong Woods, then stretch your neck looking up the ramrod-straight trunks of redwood trees into the quiet green canopy.

Distance: 2.8-mile loop

Approximate hiking time: 2 hours

Difficulty: Moderate due to elevation change

Trail surface: Dirt singletrack, pavement

Best seasons: Year-round; the dirt East Ridge Trail may be muddy during and after rainstorms

Other trail users: Equestrians

Canine compatibility: Dogs not permitted on trails; leashed dogs allowed on paved roads and in picnic areas only

Fees and permits: No fee to park in the visitor center parking lot at the park entrance; fee charged to drive into the park

Schedule: Open daily, 8:00 a.m.

to one hour after sunset

Trailhead facilities: Parking area; visitor center, restrooms, trashcans, water, information signboard

Maps: USGS Cazadero and Guerneville; brochure with map available at the visitor center; online map at www.parks.ca.gov

Other: The visitor center is open from 11:00 a.m. to 3:00 p.m. daily. Picnic facilities can be reserved by calling (707) 865-2391. Camping facilities are available in neighboring Austin Creek State Recreation Area on a first-come, first-served basis.

Trail contacts: Armstrong Redwoods State Natural Reserve/ Austin Creek State Recreation Area, 17000 Armstrong Woods

Rd., Guerneville, CA 95446; (707) 869-2015; www.parks.ca .gov. Stewards of the Coast and Redwoods, P.O. Box 2, Duncan Mills, CA 95430; (707) 869-9177; www.stewardsofthecoast andredwoods.org.

Finding the trailhead: From US 101 between Santa Rosa and Windsor, take the River Road exit. Head west on River Road for about 15 miles to the junction with Armstrong Woods Road in Guerneville. Turn right (north) onto Armstrong Woods Road and go 2.2 miles to the road's end at the park. The parking area and East Ridge trailhead are on the right. GPS: N38 31.927' / W123 0.143'

The Hike

Muir Woods National Monument without the crowds— that's what you'll find at Armstrong Woods. Towering coast redwoods, a peaceful creek, an understory softened with ferns and clover-leafed redwood sorrel, interpretive signs that describe significant trees along the route—they're all here. But given the park's location, farther off the beaten tourist path, you won't find yourself shoulder to shoulder with your fellow hiker.

The reserve is the legacy of lumberjack James B. Armstrong. In a move enlightened for the times (the late nineteenth century), Armstrong set aside this pocket of old-growth trees for posterity, protecting them from the gold rush–fed harvest that devastated so many redwood forests along the West Coast. The redwoods preserved within the park boundaries include the Parson Jones Tree, a giant at 310 feet, and the ancient Colonel Armstrong Tree, more than 1,400 years old.

The route begins on the East Ridge Trail, a dirt singletrack that ascends through a mixed evergreen forest, sometimes steeply, onto the ridge between the Fife Creek drainage and neighboring Redwood Creek. In spring look for blooming redwood sorrel, trillium, and mission bells along the trail.

Roll along the ridge for about 1.0 mile. You won't have views because of the trees, but it's a peaceful roller-coaster ramble on a broader track. A downhill pitch lands at the junction with the Picnic Area Trail, which drops quickly to Fife Creek via switchbacks. Be sure to take the short spur that leads to a bench with views of a cascade that flows in winter and spring.

Pick up the Pioneer Trail on the canyon floor. The well-groomed path weaves through dark, quiet redwood groves, and rustic bridges span the placid, meandering creek. Interpretive signs provide insight into the redwood ecosystem. Circle the Icicle Tree, with its dripping black burls, pass around and along fallen giants, and visit the General Armstrong Tree. Pick up the Braille-interpreted Discovery Trail at the General Armstrong Tree, and take the ramp up and around a redwood whose trunk has been worn smooth by touch. Finish the loop on the Armstrong Nature Trail, which leads past the impressive Parson Jones Tree and the Burbank Circle before ending at the trailhead.

Miles and Directions

0.0 Start at the signed East Ridge trailhead.

0.3 Climb around a switchback at a trail sign.

0.6 On the roller-coaster ridgetop, the trail widens to double-track. The path splits, then merges again. Stay right.

1.2 At the trail junction, go left and downhill on the Picnic Area Trail, passing a bench and creek overlook.

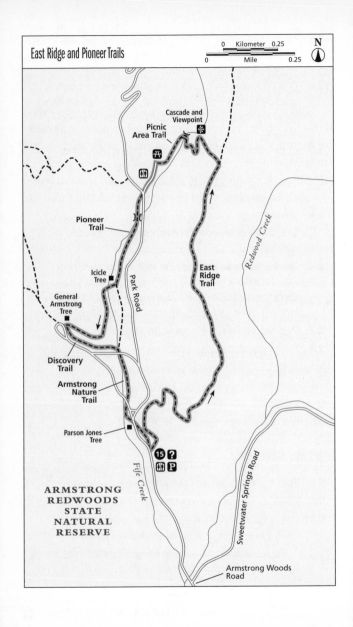

East Ridge and Pioneer Trails

0   Kilometer   0.25

0   Mile   0.25

N

Cascade and
Viewpoint

Picnic
Area Trail

Pioneer
Trail

Icicle
Tree

East
Ridge
Trail

Redwood Creek

General
Armstrong
Tree

Park Road

Discovery
Trail

Armstrong
Nature
Trail

Parson Jones
Tree

15

Fife Creek

Sweetwater Springs Road

ARMSTRONG
REDWOODS
STATE
NATURAL
RESERVE

Armstrong Woods
Road

1.4 At the unsigned trail junction, go right on the spur trail to the cascade viewpoint. Retrace your steps to the main track and go right, continuing downhill.

1.6 Cross the creek via a bridge. Enter the picnic area, with restrooms, trashcans, barbecue pits, and a volunteer center. Head left along the paved road, following the creek downstream.

1.8 At the road fork, pick up the signed, hikers-only Pioneer Trail.

2.0 Take the signed right fork for the General Armstrong Tree, passing the Icicle Tree.

2.5 Reach the General Armstrong Tree. Pick up the Discovery Trail on the south side of the tree and follow the path downstream.

2.6 Cross a park road and pass the trailhead for the Pioneer Trail. Take the Armstrong Nature Trail, which heads right. Cross the park road again at the Parson Jones Tree. Follow the path, lined with split-rail fences, past the Burbank Circle.

2.7 Pass the signed Pioneer-Nature Trail trailhead.

2.8 Arrive back at the visitor center.

16 Bodega Head

On a clear day, a tour around Bodega Head presents views of whale migration routes in the Pacific, the mouth of Tomales Bay with Point Reyes beyond, the golden arc of Doran Beach, and Bodega Harbor.

Distance: 2.1-mile loop

Approximate hiking time: 1 hour

Difficulty: Easy

Trail surface: Dirt singletrack; compacted aggregate

Best seasons: Year-round; winter winds and rains may render portions of the trail muddy and inhospitable

Other trail users: None

Canine compatibility: No dogs permitted

Fees and permits: No fees or permits required

Schedule: Open daily, sunrise to sunset

Trailhead facilities: Large parking lot; restrooms, trashcans, overflow parking along the roadside

Maps: USGS Bodega Head; Sonoma Coast State Park brochure available online at www.parks.ca.gov

Other: The trail is accessible. Hiking, camping, whale and wildlife watching, tide pooling, fishing, and picnicking are offered throughout Sonoma Coast State Park. Whale watching season is from December to April. Stewards of the Coast and Redwoods docents staff Bodega Head during whale watching season; visit www.stewardsofthecoastandredwoods.org for more information.

Special considerations: Dangerous surf and rip currents make swimming and wading along the Sonoma coast dangerous. Be prepared for cold, wet weather at any time of year.

Trail contacts: Sonoma Coast State Park, 3095 Highway 1, Bodega Bay, CA 94923; (707) 875-3483 or (707) 865-2391; www.parks.ca.gov

Finding the trailhead: From CA 1 in Bodega Bay, take East Shore Drive downhill toward the harbor for 0.3 mile. Turn right (west) onto Bay Flat Road and follow it around the bay for 3.7 miles, passing Spud Point Marina and Campbell Cove, to the parking area at road's end. GPS: N38 18.201' / W123 3.871'

The Hike

Expansive Sonoma Coast State Park stretches for 17 miles along the edge of the Pacific and includes parcels of scenic coastline from Bodega Bay north to Russian Gulch. Bodega Head, a massive buttress jutting into the bay, is at the south end of the park, and the views from its high points are simply stunning.

The accessible loop that circumnavigates the headland is pretty straightforward, circling from views of the open ocean, where you may see whales migrating in season, to the blue expanse of Bodega Bay, with the mouth of Tomales Bay and Point Reyes in the distance, to Doran Beach, the rolling coastal hills, and shimmering Bodega Harbor.

Begin by climbing the wide path to the top of the bluff above the whale watching vantage point, where you'll find the stark concrete Fishermen's Memorial. Beyond the memorial, a steep trail plunges to a tiny cove; stay safely aloft on the bluff.

Gentle climbing along the sharp edge of the headland leads to an overlook at the 0.5-mile mark, where you can enjoy views south across Bodega Bay to Point Reyes. The good gravel path circles east, looking down on a small island where barking seals sun themselves. Be sure to check out the wildflowers if you visit in spring, with bright fiddlenecks and purple iris vying for showiest bloom among the green grasses and coastal scrub.

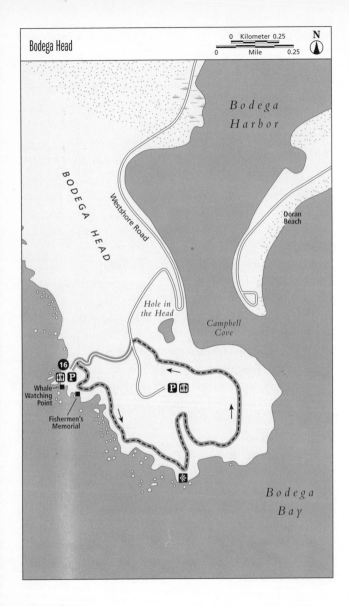

Bodega Head

Bodega Harbor

BODEGA HEAD

Westshore Road

Doran Beach

Hole in the Head

Campbell Cove

16

Whale Watching Point

Fishermen's Memorial

Bodega Bay

0   Kilometer 0.25

0   Mile   0.25

N

Round the point, now heading north, and look down on the yellow arc of Doran Beach and the blue harbor (sometimes brown, depending on the tide). The path circles to a restroom and parking lot, then passes through ceanothus and coyote brush back to the parking area and trailhead. Trail work slated to be complete by 2011 includes improvements to the last section of the route.

Options: The Hole in the Head, now a water-filled basin, is all that remains of a foiled attempt to build a nuclear plant at Bodega Head. The Hole is at the base of the switchback in the road leading up to the trailhead.

Miles and Directions

0.0 Start by climbing the path to the top of the bluff.

0.1 Pass the Fishermen's Memorial.

0.2 Pass the scary social trail down to the cove, staying left on the blufftop path. A grove of windblown cypress is on the left.

0.5 A social trail leads out to a viewpoint.

0.6 Pass another viewpoint.

0.8 Take the left (inside) trail up to the gravel path, then stay right (east). (FYI: Heading left on the gravel trail leads back toward the parking area.)

1.2 Round the point, now heading north with views of Doran Beach and Bodega Harbor. Pass a picnic table.

1.5 Pass a restroom building and closed parking area. Stay on the gravel path.

2.1 Arrive back at the trailhead.

Napa Valley

17 Napa River Trail (Kennedy Park)

The expansive Napa River floodplain, a fertile wetland that supports healthy populations of songbirds, shorebirds, and wildflowers, is the setting for this easy paved trail.

Distance: 3.0 miles out and back

Approximate hiking time: 1.5 hours

Difficulty: Easy

Trail surface: Paved

Best seasons: Year-round

Other trail users: Cyclists, runners

Canine compatibility: Leashed dogs permitted

Fees and permits: No fees or permits required

Schedule: Open daily, sunrise to sunset

Trailhead facilities: Large paved parking lots; picnic sites, restrooms, trashcans, water, playground, sporting greens

Maps: USGS Napa

Other: Plans are in place to extend the Napa River Trail from Kennedy Park to Trancas Street in the downtown area.

Trail contacts: City of Napa Parks and Recreation Department, 1100 West St., Napa, CA 94552; (707) 257-9529; www.cityofnapa.org

Finding the trailhead: From CA 29 in Napa, take the Imola Avenue exit. Follow Imola Avenue east for 1.4 miles to the Napa-Vallejo Highway (CA 221). Turn right (south) onto CA 221 and go 0.6 mile to Streblow Drive (at Napa Valley College and the Napa Municipal Golf Course). Turn right onto Streblow and go 0.5 mile to the Egret Picnic Area. GPS: N38 16.093' / W122 16.931'

The Hike

This flat, paved trail is the first leg of a planned 6.0-mile recreational path that will follow the Napa River through

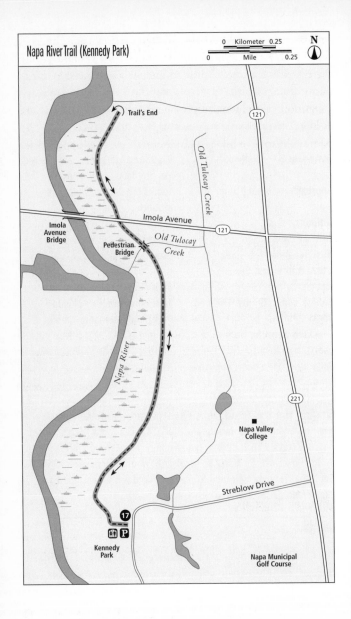

Napa River Trail (Kennedy Park)

Trail's End

Old Tulocay Creek

Imola Avenue

Imola Avenue Bridge

Pedestrian Bridge

Old Tulocay Creek

Napa River

Napa Valley College

Streblow Drive

Kennedy Park

Napa Municipal Golf Course

0   Kilometer   0.25
0   Mile   0.25

N

17

121

121

221

the downtown area. When complete, residents and visitors will be able to explore riparian zones and wetlands along the riverfront, as well as link to the city's historic sites, businesses, and restaurants.

Among the amenities planned for the linear parkway are boat launches, fishing access, and observation platforms. The path will also give hikers and other trail users an opportunity to do some quality bird watching, as marshes and riparian habitat are favorites of a variety of avian species, from red-winged blackbirds to crows to cormorants.

In the meantime, this pleasant 1.5-mile stretch is already in place. It begins in John F. Kennedy Park, the biggest in the city, boasting a boatload of recreational amenities. Wetlands stretch between the trail and the river, extending north to the Imola Avenue Bridge and beyond. The other side of the trail presents a commercial front, with parking areas, ball fields, and a solar panel installation.

The route is easy and straightforward. Follow the pavement north, looping onto a parallel dirt singletrack for a short stretch through a restoration project if you desire. A pedestrian bridge spans Old Tulocay Creek, then the trail passes beneath the concrete pillars supporting the Imola Avenue Bridge, an interesting juxtaposition of nature and development. You'll pass a couple of access points before you reach trail's end and retrace your steps to Kennedy Park.

Miles and Directions

0.0 Start by climbing a dirt track from the picnic area onto the paved trail. Turn right (north); you'll pass another trailhead parking lot within 100 feet.

0.3 A dirt trail breaks to the left, into restoration plantings and past benches placed by the local Kiwanis Club. The single-track and the pavement parallel each other.

0.4 The dirt track ends by rejoining the paved trail.

0.6 Views upriver are dominated by the Imola Avenue Bridge; a ball field is to the right, and the marsh stretches to open water. Houses and boat launches crowd the river's far shore.

0.8 Pass the trail link to Napa Valley College, staying left on the paved trail.

1.0 Cross the pedestrian bridge over Old Tulocay Creek.

1.1 Pass under the architecturally interesting Imola Avenue Bridge.

1.2 Pass another access trail, staying left on the riverside track.

1.5 The trail ends where the pavement ends, marked by a sign. Retrace your steps.

3.0 Arrive back at the trailhead.

18 Alston Park Tour

A favorite of pet owners—a section of the park is open for off-leash dog walking—this suburban park also offers treats for the hiker, including a loop that skims the borders of vineyards and offers great views.

Distance: 2.5-mile lollipop

Approximate hiking time: 1.5 hours

Difficulty: Moderate due to elevation changes and route finding challenges

Trail surface: Gravel and dirt roads, pavement, dirt singletrack

Best seasons: Spring and fall

Other trail users: Dog walkers, mountain bikers on paved trails, equestrians

Canine compatibility: Leashed dogs permitted throughout the park; dogs under voice control allowed off-leash on some trails

Fees and permits: No fees or permits required

Schedule: Open daily, sunrise to sunset

Trailhead facilities: Large dirt parking lot; information signboard (but no map), restrooms, trashcans, dog waste station, fenced dog park

Maps: USGS Napa; trail map available from the Napa Parks and Recreation Department

Special considerations: Trails are not well signed, and social paths crisscross the park, but the landscape is open enough that it is easy to stay oriented.

Trail contacts: City of Napa Parks and Recreation Department, 1100 West St., Napa, CA 94552; (707) 257-9529; www.cityofnapa.org

Finding the trailhead: From CA 29 in Napa, take Trower Avenue west for 0.9 mile to Dry Creek Road. Turn right onto Dry Creek Road, then immediately left into the parking lot. The address is 2037 Dry Creek Rd. GPS: N38 19.375' / W122 19.948'

The Hike

Alston Park is a dog's paradise. Canine companions romp the trails with their masters, relishing the rare freedom of being able to explore off-leash. Too bad most dogs keep their noses to the ground. If they bothered to look up (like their humans do), they'd find the park also boasts great views of the Napa Valley.

The 157-acre parcel is composed mostly of rolling grassland, with sparse clusters of oak offering shade. The grasses explode with wildflowers in spring and burnish gold in fall. The lack of shade can make a hike here a scorcher in the heat of a summer day. On the upside, there's nothing to block the views. Benches and picnic tables are thoughtfully placed on hilltops, good places to sit and be still.

Trails are not well marked, and social paths frequently intersect main tracks. This tour does its best to follow the Valley View Trail up onto a grassy plateau, where views open east across the valley, as well as to the north. The Valley View Trail—and associated trails—climbs to the paved service road, which leads to more wonderful views and past a fenced vineyard.

The unsigned Dry Creek Trail explores the park's high ground, skirting a wooded valley at the property line to another fenced vineyard, then dropping into the drainage of a seasonal stream. Mucky in the rainy season, the stream waters a shady stretch of oak and bay laurel and a great springtime wildflower bloom. The Jack Rabbit Trail (again unsigned) links back to the service road, which leads to the Valley View Trail and the trailhead.

While you stand a good chance of roaming off route, given the number of social paths and intersecting dirt roads, the park is small enough and open enough that you won't get lost.

Miles and Directions

0.0 Start by following the main route (Valley View, with a TRAIL sign) to a picnic site and a staircase shaded by oaks. Go right and uphill from the top of the staircase. Pass social trails, staying left on the broad track and passing a blank information signboard.

0.25 At the unsigned junction with a fire road, go right. At the next intersection (with a TRAIL sign), go right. Leave the unleashed dog zone and pass a fenceline.

0.4 Dip through drainages and pass a TRAIL sign. A cluster of oaks tops the hill to the right, where a picnic table offers views to the north. Stay left from the picnic table.

0.6 Stay left at the first junction with a side trail to the paved service road, crossing a dirt road and climbing past a water spigot and trashcan. Cross the pavement and follow a rutted dirt road up to a memory bench at the top of the hill.

0.8 Meet up with the service road (now gravel) at benches and a water tank. Go right and head west toward the wooded hills.

1.1 The trail narrows as it drops alongside a vineyard. Reach the tree-lined park boundary, where a narrow track leads left to a bench in the shade. This social path drops farther into the woods, onto private property. Stay right and climb to a trail Y at a vista bench. Stay left, following the low fence north toward the vineyard. The trail turns east at the vineyard fenceline and roller-coasters downhill, with the grapevines on the left and a grassy bowl on the right.

1.6 A steep pitch drops into a drainage, which may be soggy in winter and spring. Stay right, following the forested drainage.

1.7 Cross a bridge.

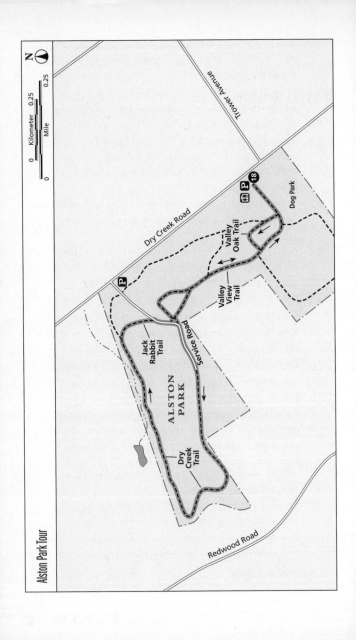

Alston Park Tour

N

0   Kilometer   0.25

0   Mile   0.25

Dry Creek Road

Trower Avenue

Valley Oak Trail

P

18

P

Dog Park

Valley View Trail

Jack Rabbit Trail

ALSTON PARK

Service Road

Dry Creek Trail

Redwood Road

1.8 Stay right at the next two trail junctions, heading uphill to meet the paved service road. Follow the pavement uphill to the next intersection.

1.9 At the junction go left on the dirt track, heading south toward the parking lot (now in sight). Do your best to retrace your steps to the trailhead.

2.5 Arrive back at the trailhead.

19 Westwood Hills Park Tour

From the highest point in this neighborhood park, views reach east across the Napa Valley, south to Mount Diablo, and west to Mount Tamalpais.

Distance: 1.2 miles out and back

Approximate hiking time: 1 hour

Difficulty: Easy

Trail surface: Dirt fire road

Best seasons: Year-round

Other trail users: None

Canine compatibility: Leashed dogs permitted

Fees and permits: No fees or permits required

Schedule: Open daily, sunrise to sunset

Trailhead facilities: Small dirt parking lot; information sign-board, portable toilet; additional parking available along Browns Valley Road

Maps: USGS Napa; map available from the Napa Parks and Recreation Department

Special considerations: Trails are not signed, and social paths crisscross the route. Explore other trails as time and experience permit.

Trail contacts: City of Napa Parks and Recreation Department, 1100 West St., Napa, CA 94552; (707) 257-9529; www .cityofnapa.org

Finding the trailhead: From CA 29, take the downtown Napa/ First Street exit. Go left on First Street (which becomes Browns Valley Road) for 1 mile to the park entrance on the left. GPS: N38 18.171' / W122 19.178'

The Hike

This neighborhood park offers about 3 miles of formal trails and a number of social trails that present opportunities for exploration (and for coming into contact with poison oak). Follow the main track through the park and you'll climb easy fire roads to a summit overlook with spectacular views—with no risk of an itchy rash later on.

The views from the summit bench are panoramic. On a clear day you can see down into Napa and east into the Vaca Mountains, south down the Napa River toward San Pablo Bay and Mount Diablo, and west to the wooded coastal mountains and Mount Tamalpais. An enviable home on the summit blocks some of the views, but they are wonderful just the same.

The route begins in a drainage shaded by stands of fragrant eucalyptus, following the unsigned Valley View Trail. Eucalyptus was brought into California from Australia as a source of lumber and firewood, as an ornamental tree, and to serve as shade and windbreaks. These days they are sometimes looked upon as weeds and nuisances, albeit attractive ones.

Valley View is one of the park's formal trails, and while there are no trail signs, it is lined with picnic sites and trashcans. Hike up the draw to a five-way trail junction, with views down and right into a meadow-filled bowl. Continue uphill, now in a native oak woodland, reaching another unsigned junction at a picnic site.

A final uphill pitch leads to the summit, an expanse of sun-splashed meadow with a single overlook bench. Take in the views, then retrace your steps to the trailhead.

If you're adventurous, you can try one of the other paths: Some are formal and sport reasonable angles on the descent; others are informal and can be knee-rattling steep.

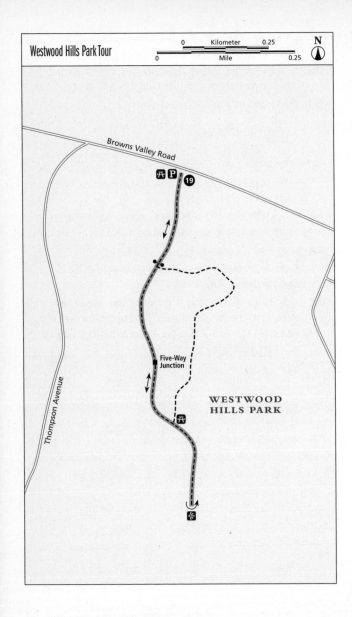

Westwood Hills Park Tour

0   Kilometer   0.25

0   Mile   0.25

N

Browns Valley Road

19

Thompson Avenue

Five-Way
Junction

WESTWOOD
HILLS PARK

Miles and Directions

0.0   Start by following the dirt path through the picnic ground and around the gate. A private residence is to the left.

0.1   Pass a second gate. At the trail junction on the other side, stay straight, ignoring trails that branch right onto the hillside and left into the drainage.

0.2   At the next junction, with a TRAIL sign, bench, and trashcan, stay straight on the dirt roadway. Looking through the eucalyptus to the left, you can see a trail that runs parallel on the other side of the drainage.

0.3   Reach a five-way trail junction at a bench. Take the track that continues straight and uphill into the oaks.

0.4   A trail arrow directs you left, up the road.

0.5   Reach a junction in a clearing with a picnic table. Go right and continue climbing.

0.6   Arrive at the summit. Take in the views, then retrace your steps. From the five-way junction you can take the trail that runs down the other side of the drainage, hooking back up with the main trail at the gate.

1.2   Arrive back at the trailhead.

20 Ritchey Canyon and Coyote Peak Trails (Bothe–Napa Valley State Park)

Though the redwood-thick shade along Ritchey Creek is the highlight of this trail loop, the high point, Coyote Peak, offers filtered views of the Napa Valley floor and the steep wooded slopes of the Mayacamas Mountains.

Distance: 5.0-mile lollipop

Approximate hiking time: 2 to 3 hours

Difficulty: More challenging due to trail length and elevation change

Trail surface: Dirt singletrack, dirt road

Best seasons: Spring through fall

Other trail users: Mountain bikers and equestrians on the Spring Trail and the multiuse portion of the Ritchey Canyon Trail

Canine compatibility: Dogs not permitted on trails; leashed pets allowed in picnic areas and the campground

Fees and permits: Day-use fee

Schedule: Open daily, sunrise to sunset

Trailhead facilities: Small parking area; information signboard, picnic table. Restrooms, water, trashcans, and other amenities available elsewhere in the park

Maps: USGS Calistoga; map in park brochure, available for a fee

Other: Other sites worth exploring in the park include the visitor center, open when staffing allows, the Native American Garden, and the Pioneer Cemetery. A dip in the swimming pool, open seasonally, is the perfect way to cool off after a hot summer hike.

Trail contacts: Bothe–Napa Valley State Park, 3801 St. Helena Hwy. North, Calistoga, CA 94515; (707) 942-4574; www.parks.ca.gov

Finding the trailhead: The park is located just west of CA 29 (St. Helena Highway), about 4 miles south of Calistoga and 3 miles north of St. Helena. Look for the signs. Follow the park road past the entrance kiosk and visitor center to the signed trailhead on the right. GPS: N38 33.117' / W122 31.135'

The Hike

Combine an easy ramble through redwood groves along Ritchey Creek with a brisk climb to the summit of Coyote Peak, and you'll understand why these are among the most popular trails in the park.

The Redwood Trail—a wide, cool, walk-and-talk path—parallels the south side of Ritchey Creek. Verdant ferns and redwood sorrel carpet the canyon floor in winter and spring. Shallow fords lead across the creek to the Ritchey Canyon Trail, which runs parallel on the opposite side, and side trails lead down to scenic streamside rest spots. The peaceful, contemplative canyon sandwiches the more challenging climb to Coyote Peak.

The Coyote Peak Trail heads up out of Ritchey Canyon into a drier forest of tan oak, madrone, manzanita, bay laurel, and Douglas fir. The route traverses above a drainage where a seasonal stream waters stands of redwoods. Cross the stream, round a switchback, and keep climbing, eventually traversing onto a scrubby west-facing slope with views into the forested folds of the Mayacamas Mountains.

The rocky spur trail to the viewpoint atop Coyote Peak is the most challenging stretch along the route. Climb the narrow track through encroaching brush to the overlook, where you can gaze eastward down through the trees into the Napa Valley and west into the mountains.

Ritchey Canyon and Coyote Peak Trails (Bothe-Napa Valley State Park)

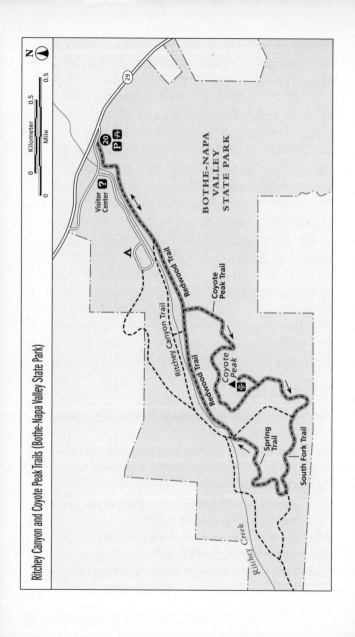

Back on the Coyote Peak Trail, a shady downhill traverse leads through a pair of seasonal stream drainages, the second in a redwood grove that rings with birdsong and the sound of falling water in winter. Listen for spotted owls, which are reported to live in the park's backcountry.

The Coyote Peak Trail ends on the South Fork Trail. The section of trail that drops to the right is an old skid road, used by lumbermen to move harvested trees. Instead of following the skid road fork, go left on a traversing track that would have stymied any lumberjack. Pass a spur trail to an overlook, then drop to the multiuse Spring Trail.

The Spring Trail leads down to the canyon floor and the junction with the upper end of the Redwood Trail. Rockhop across the creek below a big pool and under a fallen tree to pick up the singletrack Redwood Trail, then head downstream, again enveloped in redwoods. Pass another ford that leads to the Ritchey Canyon Trail and the intersection with the Coyote Peak Trail. Turn left and retrace your steps from the Coyote Peak junction to the trailhead.

Miles and Directions

0.0 Start by following the signed Ritchey Canyon Trail into the woodland.

0.1 Cross the paved road that leads to the park host's campsite, then stay left on the trail, with the creek flowing to your right.

0.2 Bear right on the Ritchey Canyon Trail.

0.5 Pass the ford. The Ritchey Canyon Trail goes right, across the creek. Stay left on the Redwood Trail.

0.9 Reach the intersection with the Coyote Peak Trail. Go left and uphill toward Coyote Peak.

1.2 Cross a stream and round a switchback, then continue to climb.

1.7 Traverse a west-facing slope with views into the Mayacamas Mountains.

1.8 Arrive at the junction with the spur to the Coyote Peak overlook. Climb to the viewpoint, take in the vistas, and then retrace your steps to the main trail.

2.0 Back at the junction, go left to continue on the Coyote Peak Trail.

2.5 At the junction with the South Fork Trail, go left.

2.8 Pass a spur to an overlook. Stay left on the South Fork Trail.

3.0 Meet the Spring Trail (a dirt road). Go right and downhill.

3.4 Pass the junction with the bottom of the South Fork Trail. Stay straight, following a short stretch of the Ritchey Canyon Trail to the Redwood Trail junction. Go right, fording the creek, onto the Redwood Trail.

4.0 Pass a ford to the Ritchey Canyon Trail, staying right on the Redwood Trail.

4.1 Pass the Coyote Peak Trail, staying left on the Redwood Trail. Retrace your steps from here.

5.0 Arrive back at the trailhead.

21 Oat Hill Mine Trail

This historic mining road leads up into the hills on the east side of the Napa Valley and offers hikers a taste of wilderness and great vineyard views.

Distance: 3.2 miles out and back

Approximate hiking time: 2 hours

Difficulty: Moderate due to elevation change

Trail surface: Dirt mining road

Best seasons: Spring and early summer

Other trail users: Mountain bikers

Canine compatibility: Dogs permitted on leash or under firm voice control

Fees and permits: No fees or permits required

Schedule: Open daily, sunrise to sunset

Trailhead facilities: Parking for two to three cars; information signboard; additional parking across the road

Maps: USGS Calistoga; map at trailhead; online at napaoutdoors.org/parks-trails/oat-hill-mine-trail

Special considerations: These hills grow parched by late summer and fall, and the upper trail may be closed when fire danger gets too high.

Trail contacts: Napa County Regional Park and Open Space District, 1195 Third St., Room 210, Napa, CA 94559; napa outdoors.org

Finding the trailhead: The trailhead is at the junction of CA 29 and the Silverado Trail west of downtown Calistoga. From the stop sign on CA 29 in Calistoga, drive 1 mile to the intersection. The trailhead is on the north side of the junction. GPS: N38 35.362' / W122 34.636'

The Hike

While the views are civilized—of orderly vineyards, glittering retention ponds, and the rooftops of rural homes—and road noise occasionally drifts up into the hills, the Oak Hill Mine Trail also feels wild and remote.

It's a wonder the road ever got built. The winding passage took twenty years to construct, linking Calistoga (and its railroad) with a cinnabar mine that operated on and off from the 1870s to the 1960s. The miners distilled quicksilver (mercury) from the cinnabar; the quicksilver in turn was used to refine gold from California's Mother Lode and silver from Nevada's Comstock Lode.

While it's hard to imagine driving wagons loaded with ore up and down the grade, for hikers the road serves as an easy route into the wooded draws below the Palisades. The route begins parallel to CA 29 but soon veers to the north and east, with views opening within 0.1 mile. The mine road links with trails in Robert Louis Stevenson State Park above and continues for more than 8.0 miles to its upper trailhead on Aetna Springs Road.

Traveling the entire trail out and back, at 16.0 miles round-trip, puts the trek well outside the realm of easy. But taking on the first 1.6 miles to an informal overlook is well within range. The road is wide and obvious, the grade gentle. Occasionally the trail surface is rocky, but it never presents a great challenge. Set a comfortable pace and you can climb for miles.

Lichens drip from the oaks along the lower portion of the trail, an indication that the air and environment is clean. In spring the green hills blush purple with vetch and lupine, the color shifting to gold as the dry season progresses. As

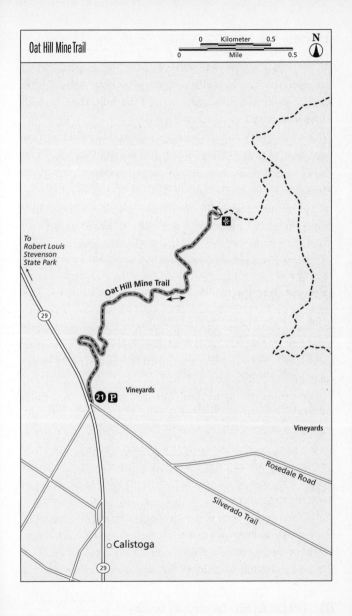

Oat Hill Mine Trail

0   Kilometer   0.5
0   Mile   0.5

N

To
Robert Louis
Stevenson
State Park

29

Oat Hill Mine Trail

21 P   Vineyards

Vineyards

Rosedale Road

Silverado Trail

Calistoga

29

it climbs, the route slips in and out of wooded drainages where valley views disappear. That's where the magic is: The hike goes wild and remote in these draws. The turnaround is a grassy knoll overlooking the valley a little beyond the 1.5-mile mark.

But continue as far as you like. You define what's easy on the Oat Hill Mine Trail—just remember to keep enough gas for the descent. Above the knoll, the trail grows rockier and is shaded by bowers of spindly manzanita. Climb to the Holms homestead site, and the trail link into the Palisades in a little more than 4.0 miles. Striking volcanic formations along the upper portions of the trail are documented in a trailside geology guide available online at napaoutdoors.org/parks-trails/oat-hill-mine-trail.

Miles and Directions

0.0 Start by climbing parallel to CA 29.

0.1 The first views—close-ups of vineyards—open up.

0.25 Stay left where a social trail breaks right up a steep pitch. (FYI: Cutting the switchback also cuts off some great views.) Cross the top of the social trail above.

0.5 Pass great downvalley views, then head into a draw where signs of civilization, including road noise, disappear.

1.2 Another social trail takes off to the left. Stay straight on the ascending roadbed. The social path rejoins the main track above.

1.6 A seep in this draw remains wet into spring and dries later in the year. Just beyond lies a pretty little knoll, with a social trail leading down through the grasses. Take in the views, then return as you came.

3.2 Arrive back at the trailhead.

22 Stevenson Monument Trail (Robert Louis Stevenson State Park)

This study in switchbacks leads to a monument erected to honor famed writer Robert Louis Stevenson, who honeymooned on the lower slopes of Mount St. Helena in 1880.

Distance: 1.4 miles out and back

Approximate hiking time: 1 hour

Difficulty: Moderate due to rocky trail surface and elevation change

Trail surface: Rocky dirt singletrack

Best seasons: Spring and fall

Other trail users: None (mountain bikers permitted on the trail to the summit of Mount St. Helena)

Canine compatibility: Dogs not permitted

Fees and permits: No fees or permits required

Schedule: Open daily, sunrise to sunset

Trailhead facilities: Dirt parking lots on both sides of CA 29

Maps: USGS Detert Reservoir; map in the park brochure, available for a fee at Bothe–Napa Valley State Park

Other: There have been auto break-ins at the trailhead parking area. Do not leave valuables in your vehicle. Mileage to the Stevenson Monument (one way) is listed as 1.0 mile on a trail sign and 0.8 mile on the trail map. The GPS mileage of 0.7 mile recorded on-site is used here.

Trail contacts: Bothe–Napa Valley State Park, 3801 St. Helena Hwy. North, Calistoga, CA 94515; (707) 942-4574; www .parks.ca.gov

Finding the trailhead: From the junction of CA 29 and CA 128 at the stop sign in Calistoga, follow CA 29 north for about 8 miles to the trailhead at the summit. GPS: N38 39.143' / W122 35.992'

Stevenson Monument Trail (Robert Louis Stevenson State Park)

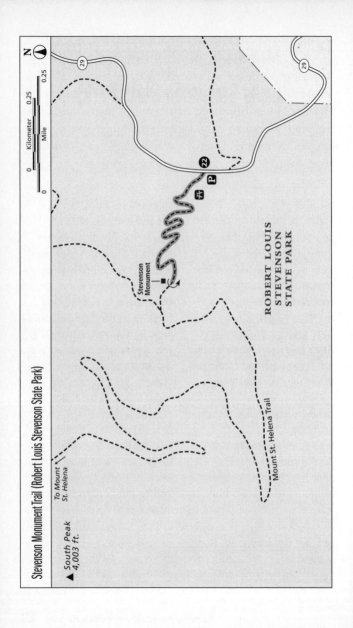

▲ South Peak
4,003 ft.

To Mount
St. Helena

Mount St. Helena Trail

ROBERT LOUIS
STEVENSON
STATE PARK

Stevenson Monument

22

P

🖼

29

29

N

0   0.25
Kilometer

0   0.25
Mile

The Hike

A small stone monument topped with an open book commemorates Robert Louis Stevenson's visit to Mount St. Helena. In the late nineteenth century, before he hit the big time, Stevenson brought his new bride, Fanny, to an abandoned mining cabin on the flanks of the mountain. Now both the cabin and Stevenson are gone, but his legacy remains.

The author of such classics as *Treasure Island, Kidnapped,* and *A Child's Garden of Verses* found inspiration on the mountain. His sojourn in what was then wilderness became the inspiration for *The Silverado Squatters.* Climb to the monument, channel the writer, and look with renewed imagination on Mount St. Helena's thick, tangled woodlands.

The trail is straightforward, climbing an easy series of switchbacks through mixed evergreen forest to a madrone- and fir-shaded clearing at the monument. Damage wrought by careless hikers cutting the switchbacks is painfully obvious, with exposed red earth streaking the mountainside like tears down a dirty cheek. Road noise precludes a backcountry experience at the trail's outset, but by the time you reach the clearing, it has been swallowed by distance and the wind in the trees.

From the monument, the trail continues to the summit of iconic Mount St. Helena, sacred to the Native Americans who once lived in the valley and site of a short-lived silver mining operation. The 5.0-mile climb is outside the realm of a best easy day hike, but experienced hikers will enjoy the trek.

Miles and Directions

0.0 From the parking lot, climb a short flight of stairs, cross the picnic area, and mount a second flight of stairs past a trail sign erroneously listing the monument as 1.0 mile distant.

0.7 End the switchbacking climb at the Stevenson Monument. Rest and relax, then retrace your steps.

1.4 Arrive back at the trailhead.

About the Author

Tracy Salcedo-Chourré has written more than twenty-five guidebooks to destinations in California and Colorado, including *Hiking Lassen Volcanic National Park, Exploring California's Missions and Presidios, Exploring Point Reyes National Seashore and the Golden Gate National Recreation Area, Best Rail Trails California,* and Best Easy Day Hikes guides to the San Francisco Bay Area, Lake Tahoe, Reno, Sacramento, Boulder, Denver, and Aspen.

Tracy is also an editor, teacher, and mom—but somehow still finds time to hike, swim, and garden. She lives with her husband, three sons, and a small menagerie of pets in California's Wine Country.

WHAT'S SO SPECIAL ABOUT UNSPOILED, NATURAL PLACES?

Beauty   Solitude   Wildness   Freedom   Quiet   Adventure
Serenity   Inspiration   Wonder   Excitement
Relaxation   Challenge

There's a lot to love about our treasured public lands, and the reasons are different for each of us. Whatever your reasons are, the national **Leave No Trace** education program will help you discover special outdoor places, enjoy them, and preserve them—today and for those who follow. By practicing and passing along these simple principles, you can help protect the special places you love from being loved to death.

THE PRINCIPLES OF **LEAVE NO TRACE**

- Plan ahead and prepare
- Travel and camp on durable surfaces
- Dispose of waste properly
- Leave what you find
- Minimize campfire impacts
- Respect wildlife
- Be considerate of other visitors

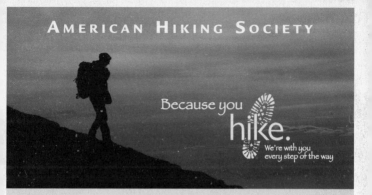